Reason in History

Reason in History

Hegel and Social Changes in Africa

Babacar Camara

LEXINGTON BOOKS
A division of
ROWMAN & LITTLEFIELD PUBLISHERS, INC.
Lanham • Boulder • New York • Toronto • Plymouth, UK

Published by Lexington Books
A division of Rowman & Littlefield Publishers, Inc.
A wholly owned subsidiary of The Rowman & Littlefield Publishing Group, Inc.
4501 Forbes Boulevard, Suite 200, Lanham, Maryland 20706
http://www.lexingtonbooks.com

Estover Road, Plymouth PL6 7PY, United Kingdom

Copyright © 2011 by Lexington Books

All rights reserved. No part of this book may be reproduced in any form or by any electronic or mechanical means, including information storage and retrieval systems, without written permission from the publisher, except by a reviewer who may quote passages in a review.

British Library Cataloguing in Publication Information Available

Library of Congress Cataloging-in-Publication Data

Camara, Babacar, 1951–
 Reason in history : Hegel and social changes in Africa / Babacar Camara.
   p. cm.
 Includes bibliographical references.
 ISBN 978-0-7391-4231-8 (cloth : alk. paper)
 1. Social change—Africa. 2. Civil society—Africa. 3. Labor—Africa—History. 4. State, The. 5. Culture. 6. Hegel, Georg Wilhelm Friedrich, 1770–1831—Political and social views. I. Title.
 HM891.C36 2011
 306.0967—dc22
                                                    2010039532

The paper used in this publication meets the minimum requirements of American National Standard for Information Sciences—Permanence of Paper for Printed Library Materials, ANSI/NISO Z39.48-1992.

Printed in the United States of America

In memory of:

Nouhoum Camara

Lopi (Pape Ndiaye Blondin Diop)

and Cheikhou Bah Coulibaly

Contents

Foreword		ix
Preface		xi
Introduction		xv
1	History According to Hegel	1
2	Contradictions in the Hegelian System	31
3	The State and Civil Society	43
4	Fundamental Aspects of African Cultures	65
5	From the Concept of Labor to the Labor of Concept	79
6	Labor in Traditional Africa	103
Epilogue		121
Bibliography		125
Index		131
About the Author		137

Foreword

Like Josef Dietzgen (1828-1888), tanner and philosopher, author of *L'essence du travail intellectuel humain* [*The Positive Outcome of Philosophy: The Nature of Human Brainwork letters on logic*, 1906], I anticipate some objections.

I foresee attacks on my lack of erudition, which is detectable within the lines that I have written, or my feeble attempts to understand the master thinker of Berlin. I ask ourselves: "How dare I write on a topic that has been dealt with by the giants of knowledge such as Aristotle, Kant, Fichte, Hegel, Marx, Pierre Franklin Tavares, and Amady Aly Dieng, among many others, without knowing in depth the work of all my predecessors? In the best-case scenario, am I not going to just repeat what they have said before me? My answer is that it has been a long time since the philosophical seed has been planted; it has grown and produced fruits. What history produces, develops itself historically, is born, grows up, and disappears to always survive in a new form.

The original work, which is the first act, is fecund only in its relation to the situation and context of the time that gave it birth, but with time, it is only an empty shell that has given its substance to history. The positive elements—the products of past knowledge—no longer reside in the letters authors form, but more than a spirit, they have become flesh and blood in today's knowledge.

To know the results of physics and find some novelties in the field, it is not indispensible to study the history of such a science and go back to the sources so far discovered. That is how I explain the lack of erudition to my advantage and thus, I am more attached to the knowledge of my own topic. I have put in a great deal of effort to study it and to use a lot of what has been said so far in my time. The history of philosophy repeats itself in me in the sense that from youth, I have begun to speculate, possessed by a need for a conception of a global world in which we have finally found satisfaction in the inductive knowledge of the human activity of thinking. It is not about the ability to think in its diverse manifestations or its different modes. What pleases us is its more general and universal essence, and that is the object of my concern today. Therefore, our topic is as banal and as particular as possible.

During our research, I have come across brilliant minds and specialists in the field, and all capable of admirable gymnastics of the mind. However, the problem of the nature of the spirit is a popular theme, which does not solely fall within the competence of philosophers or Hegel specialists, but within knowledge in general. As an author, I know that I am not a philosophy Professor but one of comparative literature. Therefore, to those who feel the need to remind us of the old saying, "Each one to his or her own trade," I respond with Karl Marx: "Ne sutor ultra crepidam—this nec plus ultra of handicraft wisdom became sheer nonsense, from the moment the watchmaker Watt invented the steam-engine, the barber Arkwright, the throttle, and the working-jeweler, Fulton, the steamship" (458-59).

Preface

Let us begin by clarifying the topic of Hegel and social change in Africa. My initial desire was to discuss the problem of change in Africa from a contemporary point of view. I wanted to use Marxist lenses or more precisely historical materialism to show that true social change in Africa, before anything, implies on the one hand that Africans themselves rely on their own strength in terms of their continent's internal and social dynamism; on the other hand, they should end the calls for external interventions or aid, given the fact that, in any case, nations beset by profound and internal contradictions can never be free. On the contrary, they must free themselves or run the risk of being granted a formal and ineffective freedom. Such a situation only plunges and maintains the people in lethargy and political unconsciousness, thus exposing them to all forms of domination and exploitation.

Following this path would have moved me away from a scholarly philosophical preoccupation. That is why I am giving my discussion a philosophical trend while still trying to maintain the initial desire. Therefore, I would like to focus on the more modest task of clearing the ground on which the problematic of change in Africa is taking place. I want to discuss the theoretical legitimacy of the notion of social change as it relates to African realities. From this standpoint, we realize that it is Hegel that deals the most with the inexistence of change in Africa. It is precisely the need to expose his so-called theses on Africa and at least show the historicity of African societies—which at the same time implies that there is an internal autonomy in African structures—that I have chosen to deal with Hegel and Africa. We have to criticize Hegel's *Philosophy on World History*, and show its contradictions as much as possible.

However, after seeing early attempts at criticizing Hegel's theses on Africa in the details like Pierre Quillet's "Hegel et l'Afrique" (1976) and other scholars who want to refute Hegel's every misrepresentations of Africa and its people, I have decided not to go that way. That kind of criticism meant a lot at the time but now it feels like grocery store labor. Now, new research has surfaced: the

Cape Verdean scholar Tavares's Ph.D. thesis (1990) and subsequent articles on Hegel and the Senegalese Dieng's new position on Hegel and his comprehensive analysis of Tavares's work (2006) have developed almost irrefutable arguments in favor of Hegel not being a racist, and having never withdrawn from the task of theorizing humanity's total freedom.

Tavares's work has been popularized by the prolific and relentless socially committed Professor Dieng. Years ago, Dieng shared the opinion that Hegel is racist. However, he has lived long enough to find material that has helped him adjust his theories. His encounter with Tavares's work has not only opened his eyes but has also set him on the path of reviewing or re-reading all the famous African writings on philosophy, Africanity, and Hegel. His *Hegel et l'Afrique* seems to need better editing, but is very comprehensive and does provide all the detailed sources and major arguments that Tavares makes about Hegel. Moreover, he sets himself the task of going through the many nuanced arguments of remote sympathizers or anti-Hegelian African scholars. He explains and criticizes the theory of all these famous African philosophers. Tavares's and Dieng's works are quite welcome for they open the door to the beginning of a long overdue and true criticism of Hegel and Africa, which should also reveal itself as a criticism of the world.

I have decided to first go to the source and review Hegel's *Philosophy of History*. After all this time, so many scattered versions, excerpts, and explanations are offered, sometimes in a "word of mouth" style. Then, I raise the few obvious contradictions in Hegel's theory. Finally, I juxtapose Hegel's position on various subjects to what we consider to be the African case. I am hoping that the reader will see that Hegel's theories ultimately do Africa justice. A closer scrutiny reveals that his ideas do acknowledge the true reality of traditional African societies. The reader will enjoy the information on Africa provided from a dialectic point of view and see that indeed there is a social dynamic in Africa. Therefore, it is not and has never been static. The reader will also notice that I am on Hegel's side and that every time and as soon as I get the opportunity, I have taken it to approve or support Hegel's thinking.

Thus, I do not tackle the issue at the same level as some scholars who may share the same general critical intentions that I have. In their global perspective, they have found the necessity to criticize Hegel as long as he denies rationality to Africans. What is important to note here is that their criticisms are more concerned with the content of African thought than with the historical evolution of Africa.

This book has profited indirectly from the encouragement and intellectual stimulation of the always inspiring Professor Sante Matteo, a mentor, colleague, and friend who is never afraid of thinking. Thank you for your editorial input.

I would like to thank Professor John Heyda, colleague, friend, and former neighbor for all the lunchtime discussions and his help with corrections of the manuscript.

I thank the staff at Lexington Books, a division of Rowman & Littlefield Publishers, Inc.

Many thanks to *Les Presses de l'Université Laval* for allowing me to use portions of Professor Kamdem's "Temps et travail en Afrique." It is a pleasure to find out that *Les Presses* abound with multidisciplinary research on Africa.

I extend my thanks to my colleagues Brian Domino and John Tassoni for helping with corrections. Thank you Professor Alan Cady for the scientific input.

Finally, I would like to thank my wife Deborah and our three sons Cheiku, Gamby, and Fily for their continued support and understanding in helping me put the manuscript together and accomplish my intellectual work.

Translations from French are the author's.

Introduction

According to the works of Cheikh Anta Diop, John Henry Clarke, Basil Davidson, Paul Bohannan, Philip Curtain, Colin Turnbull, and most Africanist scholars, Black African societies were advanced, and at an early age occupied the frontline in the march of civilization, long before the Arabs and Europeans came to the continent. Medieval Africa—which chronologically does not correspond to the European Middle Ages—was marked by a period of strong political stability due to the development of great empires and civilizations. The West African empires of Ghana (400-1240), Mali and Songhai (1200-1591) were synonymous with prosperity and splendor, known throughout the world. Other parts of Africa such as the eastern city-states of Sofala, Kilwa, and Mombasa (1200-1800) as well as the central kingdoms of Congo (1400-1600) and the southern kingdom of Monomotapa (1500-1800), were also known for their achievements and wealth. Elaborate government organizations, political stability, and trade led to wealth, knowledge, and culture in empires as well as in city-states throughout the continent.

However, the search for gold, land, and other resources led the Arabs—from the eleventh century—and Europeans, from the fifteenth century—to eventually establish a system of slavery. Hegel may not have witnessed this "civilized" Africa but could have read about it from fourteenth-century Tunisian social scientist Ibn Khaldun (1332-1406) and the Moroccan scholar and chronicler Ibn Battuta (1302-1368). As Charles d'Hondt and Dieng explain, Hegel was an avid reader. Yet, he finds the need to stress the so-called fundamentally static and therefore unhistorical character of African societies. I believe that there is a need for explanation.

Today, the inexorable progress of globalization is witnessing an Africa completely turned upside down, thus revealing the seeds planted by foreign domination centuries ago. Most of modern Africa's conflicts have been inherited from Arab and European imperialism and colonization. As a result of the arbitrary borders they have created to suit their needs, ethnic groups or nations were divided in order to weaken them according to the old strategy of "divide and conquer." After 1960, the date of independence for most African countries, some of these ethnic groups have tried to regroup and this is the source of most border conflicts.

The Rwandan genocide is an illustration of century-old ethnic antagonisms that have resurfaced in many countries after the Europeans "left." Conflicts over basic resources such as water, access and control over rich minerals and other resources, and various political agendas are among the many reasons why seven nations in the Democratic Republic of Congo (former Zaire) are engaged in endless and bloody fighting. The conflict has been fueled and supported by various national and international corporations and other regimes, which have an interest in the outcome of the conflict. The Second Congo War, beginning in 1998, is sometimes referred to as the "African World War." Despite the signing of peace accords in 2003, fighting continues in the east of the country. The war is the world's deadliest conflict since World War II, having killed 5.4 million people.

The Eritrean-Ethiopian War took place from May 1998 to June 2000, forming one of the conflicts in the Horn of Africa. Eritrea and Ethiopia spent hundreds of millions of dollars on the war and suffered the loss of tens of thousands of their citizens killed or wounded as a direct consequence of the conflict, which resulted in minor border changes.

In Niger, the Second Tuareg Rebellion began in February 2007 in parts of the Sahara desert, which detains some of the largest uranium deposits. The Tuareg group Niger Movement for Justice (NMJ) started the uprising, which aims for greater economic development and a share in the region's mineral wealth, as they proclaim. The group came to international attention after they launched attacks against government and foreign interests in northern Niger.

The scramble for Africa hit the region in the late nineteenth century when Spain was awarded the region at the 1884 Berlin Conference. As a result, Western Sahara became known as Spanish Sahara. In 1975, Morocco organized the Green March, a mass demonstration of 350,000 unarmed citizens who traveled from all parts of Morocco to the region. As a result, Spain withdrew and signed the Madrid Accords with Morocco and Mauritania, who divided the region between them. Western Sahara remains a disputed territory between Morocco and the armed guerillas of the Polisario, a nationalist organization. Since that date, Morocco claims sovereignty based on historical ties with the region while the Polisario Front claims it is an occupied territory and seeks independence in the name of the Saharawi Republic. The dispute is pending resolution.

Thus, from simple border conflicts to ethnic or civil wars, without forgetting the liberation movements and coups, the whole continent—through multiple and profound contradictions—is paying the price for having been brutally introduced to a capitalist mode in which all relations are mediated by money and merchandise.

Our task is not simple. We need to criticize Hegel's theses on Africa—in a more comprehensive way than we have done in my "The Falsity of Hegel's Theses on Africa" (2005)—and raise the theoretical issue of social change in Africa. If some thinkers believe in the possibility of change in Africa, they expect it to come from outside as if the continent does not have an internal dynamism. That is why it is necessary to classify what is meant by social change before addressing it in Africa.

Society always implies a structural totality based on human activities in all their forms. If so, we cannot but consider its possible change from a structural form; thus, alterations in secondary aspects define themselves as symptoms of a more fundamental modification of the structures. Nevertheless, let us confine ourselves to this restrictive definition, i.e. society understood as a structural totality. Now the problem is to see whether society as a global structure is thereby necessarily compelled to change. In other words, we need to know whether there can be no change in social structures or on the contrary, whether any social structure implies an internal dynamism, which forms the concrete basis for any change.

What do we mean by the concept of social change? It essentially refers to an initial process of partial modifications that gradually become structural and global. Therefore, social change means de-structuration and restructuration of a determined social totality. In his *German Ideology* (1845-1846), Marx provides a striking example of the passage from feudalism to capitalism. Such a transition reveals itself in the growing preponderance of towns over countryside, commerce and industry over land labor, and serfs over former lords. It resulted in a radical process of profound transformations of a society until then founded on the domination and exploitation of peasants by a religious and warlike aristocracy. The present capitalist system thus stems from such a gradual social process.

In all this, I want to stress the fact that a society cannot really change unless it is internally affected within its profound structures. The internal basis of feudalism was the extortion of serf labor by the nobility and the clergy. With the disappearance of such a state of facts, feudalism disappears to make way for the capitalist system whose intrinsic foundations were already visible with the rise of industry and commerce.

Nevertheless, the elements determining the forms and laws of social changes are less interesting than the possibility of change itself. We need to know to what extent change is universal or just a property of a certain type of social totality. More particularly, has there ever been or can there be a structural change that would thereby reveal an internal dynamic in African societies? According to Hegel's theses in his *Philosophy in History*, there is no doubt that Africa is impervious to any social change.

His theses on Africa have given rise to so many reactions, all diverse, depending on one's social or cultural background. In general, the theses have been welcomed with a certain enthusiasm and a manifest agreement in Europe. They have also aroused condescendence from many White people who consider Africans inferior. It is almost as if Hegel has provided them with a good consciousness to justify imperialism and colonization practices in Africa. On the African scene, it tricked some Africanist thinkers to give credence to the notion of a structural specificity as elaborated in Léopold Sédar Senghor's (1906-2001) work. Apparently, the only difference here is that by affirming a so-called absolute specificity of Africa, Hegel tried to deduce a structural lethargy and a lack of civilization in Africa as showed in the first chapter; while African intellectuals who oppose Hegel have seen in his theses all the elements they need to affirm and justify the existence of a specific African civilization, which is irremediably opposed to the European one. Their goal led them to "essentialize" African realities and thereby ended up rooting them to the spot.

In one way or another, Hegel's theses on Africa have left no one indifferent. Among African students, the theses arouse a boundless wave of indignation and a systematic *a priori* condemnation. As for Black scholars in the Diaspora, most of them reject Hegel for how he ignominiously and grotesquely denigrates Blacks/Africans.

In terms of criticism, many anti-Hegelian intellectuals—consciously or not—orient the debate towards an understanding that gives a purely racist meaning to Hegel's theses. In so doing, they call for an exclusive racial consideration, thus occulting the true level of critical analysis that the theses require. For us, even if somehow the problem does imply a consideration of race, it is nevertheless more global. Hegel talks not only about Negroes but also and above all about Africa, which represents their ambient milieu. Therefore, the analysis must be aimed more at the milieu and the African social structures—be they invariable or not—rather than aimed at racial considerations, even if they are important.

Chapter 1 offers a reading of Hegel's view on history and the distinction that he makes between historical and unhistorical societies. Chapter 2 reveals some obvious contradictions in the Hegelian system as it relates to Africa. Chapter 3 discusses Hegel's and Marx's concept of the state, and the state in the particular case of Africa. Chapter 4 deals with some characteristics that could be understood as proper to African thought, arts, and languages. Chapter 5 explores the crucial notion of labor according to Hegel and Marx and the ensuing issue of alienation. Chapter 6 exposes labor in Africa in quite a Hegelian approach.

For Hegel's main references, I have used Johannes Hoffmeister's *Lectures on the Philosophy of World History* (1984), translated by H. B. Nisbet; *La raison dans l'histoire* (2007), translated by Kostas Papaioannou; *The Phenomenology of Mind* (1967), translated by J. B. Baillie; *Phénoménologie de l'esprit* (1939-1941), translated by Jean Hyppolite; *Phenomenology of the mind* (1977) and *Hegel's Science of Logic* (1969), translated by A. V. Miller; *Philosophy of Right* (1967), translated by T. M. Knox; *Principes de la philosophie du droit*, translated by André Kaan; and *Lectures on the Philosophy of Religion, Together with a Work on the Proofs of the Existence of God, Volume II*, translated by the Rev. E. B. Speirs, B. D. and J. Burdon Sanderson.

I have often been compelled to ply between versions because some translations—mostly into English—omit passages. Many times, I have also been led to provide ample quotations to render fully the quoted authors' concepts or positions. Shorter quotes would have been superficial, considering the dialectic approach that we want to maintain.

Chapter One

History According to Hegel

Hegel's philosophy no doubt represents the most radical critique of classical metaphysics. Immanuel Kant had already started such a criticism by stating the impossibility of seizing truth beyond phenomena. Kant offers a double split between on the one hand the knowing subject and on the other the real, which is external for him. He makes the distinction between two worlds: the one we experience at the rational level (the world of phenomena) and the underlying reality behind it at the sensitivity level (the world of noumena). In his *Critique of Pure Reason* (1781), Kant explains that we cannot know reality as it is. We can only know reality as organized by human understanding. The thing-in-itself is forever inaccessible. Whatever exists other than mental phenomena or ideas appearing to the mind is a thing-in-itself and cannot be directly and immediately known. Kant's transcendental idealism consists of taking a point of view outside of and above oneself (transcendentally) and understanding that the mind directly knows only phenomena or ideas.

Nevertheless, Kant's theory of knowledge remains ambiguous. His understanding is that reason beyond experience only leads to vain speculations. Although devastating, his criticism of classical metaphysics leads to more insidious metaphysics, beginning with his own transcendental idealism. He theorizes that neither reason by itself nor sensation by itself can give us knowledge of the external world. Knowledge is the result of the interaction between the mind and sensation. Knowledge and experience are shaped, structured, or formed by special regulative ideas. Kant thus separates humanity in several ways from the world or thing-in-itself and locates the perfectible parts of humanity in a rational faculty that is battling the forces of the body and the sensible truth.

If reason cannot seize the truth, it goes without saying that truth can only be apprehended by feeling and faith. The spirit resumes its position and this time, with more rigor and strength. It becomes that tangible, static, eternal reality, which is perfect in its form as well as in its essence. The important thing is not that the spirit can be seized or not, but that it simply is, and this independently of an ephemeral and indeed illusory world. With such an incapable reason, the transcending of the ceiling of eternal ideas becomes more manifest. Human beings have only to recognize such transcendence and accept that between them and the divine there is an abyss that they can only fill up with their submission. Thus, there is a spirit forever perfect and eternal facing a material world forever imperfect and perishable. In such a case, morality becomes possible because humans have the capacity to be freely willing to act according to reason. But reason essentially dictates only one law: perform only those actions whose policy can be universalized as laws of nature. However, Kant's moral philosophy gives no method of choosing between moral or immoral acts. There is an ever perfect and eternal spirit standing opposite a world forever imperfect and perishable, in which human beings are both angels and beasts, and docile moderators.

It is against such a conception that Hegel stands. Béatrice Longuenesse (2007) explains what Hegel understands by reason: "What for Kant was reason in its most rigorously pure sense (practical reason) is for Hegel the extreme manifestation of the limited standpoint of the understanding. On the other hand, what for Kant was the exercise of the understanding is for Hegel 'the true concept of reason,' that is, at least the *embryo* of reason in its true definition" (193). For Hegel thus, the spirit is no longer to be considered a disembodied and immediately self-sufficient realty. There is no distinct spirit facing a distinct world. The material world—nature—can no longer be considered a rational system. Since it is characterized by a perpetual and progressive change, one must conclude that such a change is a fundamental characteristic of the spirit. Therefore, there is no more irremovable spiritual reality that is once and for all defined. The movement of nature and society can only be understood as an expression of the spirit's development. This development does not at all exclude the intrinsic perfection, which animates the spirit.

However, such a perfection is first in itself a potentiality in the form of a latent perfection that tends to actualize itself by realizing itself as freedom. Hegel says:

> When the spirit strives towards its center, it strives to perfect its own freedom; and this striving is fundamental to its nature. To say that spirit exists would at first seem to imply that it is a completed entity. On the contrary, it is by nature active, and activity is its essence; it is its own product, and is therefore its own beginning and its own end. Its freedom does not consist in static being, but in a constant negation of all that threatens to destroy freedom. (48)

It goes without saying that this sensation of freedom finds its fundamental ground of realization in society. Hegel explains: "The spirit's own consciousness must realize itself in the world; the material or soil in which it is realized is none other than the general consciousness, the consciousness of the nation. This consciousness encompasses and guides all the aims and interests of the nation, and it is on it that the nation's rights, customs, and religion depend" (52). Therefore, world history is nothing but the history of the spirit in development. The progress of the spirit goes through a process of negativity. The spirit moves within its own internal contradictions, and universal history is only the reflection of that process of contradictions. Through such a process, the spirit reaches a more and more developed level of consciousness, mastery, and plenitude of itself. It goes through successive and evolutionary stages that reflect and manifest themselves through equally progressive social forms.

The Stages of the Spirit in Development

The spirit—universal reason—consists of three stages that represent the various levels in the process of the spirit's realization as the achieved totality or the Absolute spirit.

The Idea is first unconscious of itself as an autonomous reality perfect in itself; but it is immersed in nature, unconscious of its radical difference from it. The Idea thus remains sunken in the immediacy of existence. Hegel says: "This natural spirit is still immersed in nature and is not yet self-sufficient; it is therefore not yet free, and has not undergone the process by which freedom comes into being" (130). The spirit expresses itself through a unique individuality and in so doing imposes its tyranny onto the others who blindly obey as children would towards their fathers. The state, in such a context, is not that concrete universal through which the spirit fully develops itself by realizing individual beings' aspirations in their totality. Therefore, nations in which that spirit manifests itself are by no means historical, for they have not developed the consciousness of their freedom.

However, the spirit, by its own nature, is dynamic and evolutionary: its progressive realization implies dialectic and contradictory stages of alienation and liberation. That is why, at this purely natural stage, it does not stand still. It gets to the point when, conscious of its freedom, the spirit stands in opposition to nature. It sees in nature only a reflection, a material to dominate and master for the realization of its freedom proper. It is the objective stage in its first phase: the consciousness of freedom remains substantial and more sentimental than rational. The spirit feels that it is going well beyond the natural bounds and can only foresee or sense the necessity to radically oppose nature. This phase represents the youthful age of the spirit, which still perceives only its difference with nature. At this stage, the individual, as a representative of the spirit, has not yet attained manhood. Hegel says: "As soon as man emerges as a human being, he stands in opposition to nature, and it is this alone that makes him a human being. But if he has merely made a distinction between himself and nature, he is still at the first stage of his development: he is dominated by passion, and is nothing more than a savage" (177). Nevertheless, here, there exists the consciousness of a possible humanization through the consciousness of freedom, which leads to the second phase of the objective spirit.

Individuals thus, begin to mark their neat opposition to nature as freedom reaches a more rational than simply sentimental level. This is the spirit's manhood. Individuals, families' particular social organizations, and states get to the point where they perceive the necessity of the *State*. Such individuals, by aspiring to freedom, find it to be abstract in the frame of one's individuality; contradictions in the various individual aspirations lead to the impossibility of satisfying individuals, even if such contradictions contain the universal in themselves, although in an abstract manner. That is when, through a transcending process, the State appears as universal, merging all the individual aspirations, and sets itself the task of concretizing them. The state, defined as such, is the embodiment of the Absolute spirit or universal reason. The subordination of individuals to this state is the condition by which they realize their concrete freedom. It is the triumph of rationality and the domination of nature through a process of objectification. The objective spirit then stands in radical opposition to the subjective spirit and Reason opposes feelings and passions.

However, this stage is in-itself a mere beginning toward freedom, for as long as the contradiction between objective and subjective remains, the spirit does not attain the full consciousness of itself, which is real freedom. Such a contradiction immerses the spirit, alienates it, and makes it perceive its being only in relation to its opposition to nature. The suppression of such an opposition to nature becomes the condition then for the spirit to seize itself without any mediation. The contradiction has become interference for the spirit to free itself from artificial naturalness. Such a contradiction reveals itself as a split, an internal tear of the spirit, and in so far as it only appears "in the Absolute laceration."

Thus, a process of dialectic transcendence allows the spirit to arrive at a direct and full consciousness of itself and, in so doing, at the plenitude of its essence. The spirit then, contemplates itself in all its perfection. Having realized the synthesis of in-itself and for-itself, the spirit finds a perfected totality, which has to only embrace its proper process of perfection from within. It then reveals itself as the Absolute knowledge having itself for object. That direct and total consciousness defines the Absolute spirit. Therefore, history, which is only the unfolding of the concept aiming at its own comprehension, ends with its accomplished goal.

We are discussing here whether history has an end or not. However, we want to simply retain the following: nations are differently determined and they correspond to the various stages of the spirit's development: each nation has its own spirit, which reflects a stage of the universal spirit's evolution. Is this correspondence in-itself definite or structural? Would the development of the spirit be determined from a comparison and a gradation of nations from inferior to superior, non-civilized to civilized? If so, there certainly is a contradiction of principle to be addressed in the Hegelian system: dialectic would be pure appearance.

The movement of what Hegel calls the Absolute spirit would be the simple movement of human consciousness, which, with its cultural prejudices, classifies in its own way the historical matter.

I will certainly have to come back to this issue. For now, let us say that for Hegel world history and the history of nations are the manifestation of the history of the spirit realizing itself. Such a finding precisely leads Hegel to make a neat distinction between historical and unhistorical societies.

General Conditions on Determining the Consciousness of Nations

Conscious nations are those in which the light of the spirit—in its domination of nature and integral seizure of itself—has emerged. Such a spiritual revelation obeys precise conditions, such as the geographical basis and the climate context. Here, Hegel's position is more nuanced. For him, humans, and therefore the spirit they embody, remain tied to the sensuous world as long as they have not reached a full consciousness of themselves, through the realization of freedom. He says:

> The various national spirits are separated in time and space; and in this respect, the influence of the natural context, the relationship between the spiritual and the natural (i.e. the national temperament, etc.) makes itself felt. Seen against the universality of the ethical whole and its own active individuality, this relationship is a purely external one; but as the ground on which the spirit moves, it is nevertheless an essential and necessary basis. (152)

There are two aspects of this natural element: the subjective naturalness, which expresses the natural will of the people, and the objective and external naturalness, i.e., geography and climate. These two aspects are intrinsically connected, and a nation's character can be determined by its geographical basis, assigned by the spirit. At this point, we are tempted to talk about a certain materialism in Hegel that makes the geographical basis determinant and fundamental. We are also tempted—independently of such a position—to affirm that there is a certain "occasionalism": the people's spirit, and therefore the particular dimension of the Absolute, developing itself according to a determined natural environment. Indeed these two affirmations seem well supported when Hegel says: "It is not our business to acquaint ourselves with the nation's environment as an external locality, but merely with the natural type to which the latter belongs; for this is intimately connected with the type and character of whatever nation is rooted in this particular soil" (153).

However, it is as if Hegel refutes such affirmations beforehand. He says: "But we must not assume that the relationship of dependence between man and nature and the character of a nation is formed exclusively by the natural characteristics of its environment" (153). Before emerging in history in a natural form, spirits are already predetermined by the Idea: nature itself is only the external product of the idea, which forms the basis of everything. Thus, one should not at all give nature, or more precisely geography and climate, too strong a role in determining the spirit of a nation. This spirit, in its particularity, is not an abstraction devoid of content but a particular form of the Absolute spirit, while nature is a negative determinant. In its stand against the freedom of the spirit in itself, nature makes it actualize its latent perfection by a process of negating every opposition.

However, this is only a particularity in natural determinism. When nature is such that it does not constitute a constraint to the spirit, the spirit is taken in its latent essentiality and by no means aims at dominating nature. Therefore, depending on the specificity of the geo-climatic areas, one can determine where the spirit has begun a historical process of self-realization and where it has not done so. Let us mention beforehand that the spirit hardly uses extremes to realize itself. Therefore, in regions that are too hot or too cold, too mountainous or too arid, the spirit barely shows through, if at all. Hegel says: "Extreme conditions are not conducive to spiritual development. *Aristotle* has long since observed that man turns to universal and more exalted things only after his basic needs have been satisfied. But neither the torrid nor the frigid zones permit him to move freely, or to acquire sufficient resources to allow him to participate in higher spiritual interests" (155).

The Absolute spirit thus, despite its state of in-itself, determines nature in its yet necessary process of self-realization. We can then ask ourselves how the Absolute spirit can let itself be dominated and indeed neutralized by nature. For now, that will not be an issue. At this point, I would like to take a brief look at Hegel's historical societies from the general considerations we have provided.

Historical Societies

Historical societies are those in which the light of the spirit has emerged. From an essentially geo-climatic point of view, they are determined by their specific situation in the temperate zone. Thus, after having carved up this zone into subzones, with the northern part being the true scene of universal spirit, Hegel nevertheless states that we should not be carried away by the diversity of these subzones:

> If we now consider those determinate differences, which have a bearing on the distinct characteristics of national spirits, it should be remembered that we must confine ourselves to such essential and universal distinctions as necessary to thought and at the same time founded in empirical reality. For determinateness must be distinguished from mere diversity, which is in some measure contingent. To isolate these determining differences is the task of philosophical enquiry, and we must take care not to lose ourselves in formless diversity. (156)

Hegel thus goes as far as to consider climate and geography in certain areas as unworthy of our preoccupation because they are not decisive. He distinguishes three moments that are essential in summarizing all the determinations. The uplands represent the nomad countries. They are of an impulsive and disperse spiritual nature, without a consciously determined goal. Then we have the broad river valleys, formed by major rivers. It is here that centers of civilizations first arose. Hegel describes them: "The river plains are the most fertile lands. Agriculture becomes established there and with it, the rights of communal existence are introduced. The fertile soil automatically brings about the transition to *agriculture*, and this in turn gives rise to understanding and foresight" (158-59). They are thus the countries of transition where creativity slowly develops.

However, with this sedentary life, land and property possessions and social class divisions appear. With the institution of the determination of property and justice, a spirit of universality appears with a universal sovereign and the rule of law. Great empires and powerful states emerge in these countries. This goes beyond the nomad impulse. This process of adherence to the universal is a characteristic proper to the kingdoms located on the banks of the rivers of China, the Ganges, the Indus, and the Nile. The land owes its property to the rivers and basins that compel populations to gather around and to form powerful nations such as Ancient Egypt and its Nile valley.

The third division is that of the coastal zone, connected to the sea. Hegel says: "The *sea* in fact always gives rise to a particular way of life. Its indeterminate elements give us an impression of limitlessness and infinity; and when man feels himself part of this infinity, he is emboldened to step beyond his narrow existence" (160). More precisely, the limitlessness and infinite character of the sea suggests to humans the idea that the finitude of the terrestrial element is not suitable as long as they seek the Absolute. Courage, cunning, and intelligence are sharper in the spirit that wants to master such an innocent but destructive element that is the sea. Such a movement is not mechanical and the sea does not necessarily develop such possibilities. Asian nations for instance do not consider the sea in-itself. They only see it in relation to the land: the sea is the ultimate termination of the land.

From these geo-climatic determinations, one can find four northern types that would represent—to varying degrees—the essential in historical societies: the Orient, Greece, Rome, and German society.

The Oriental world still keeps largely something purely natural. Here, the necessity of an opposition to nature is simply glimpsed at, which allows the apparition of consciousness in-itself and for itself. This universalizing consciousness creates a strong enough connection between individual consciences, allowing thus the emergence of a state, from an ethical point of view. However, such a state, by its own essence, can only be a despotic one. The universal spirit, subjectively felt, is practically perceived only through an individuality, which thereby exercises a supreme power over the whole nation. Subjects do not see themselves as many particular and necessary liberties. They are still caught in the historical contingency and therefore lack the individual necessity to rise up to the universal. It is only through the despot or the patriarch that universality is felt as concrete. Thus, consciousness first emerges in the Oriental world. Hegel says:

> Thus, it is in Asia that the ethical world of political consciousness first arose. Asia is the continent of sunrise and of origin in general. Admittedly, every country is both east and west in relation to others, so that Asia is the western continent from the point of view of America; but just as Europe is the centre and end of the Old World—i.e. absolutely the west—so also is Asia absolutely the east. It is there that the light of the spirit, the consciousness of a universal, first emerged, and with it the process of world history. (190-91)

This consciousness in Asia is limited to the sole intuition of a universality of the spirit, without leading to a labor that actualizes such consciousness. It is precisely this intuitive mode of knowing the spirit that forms the basis of all knowledge in the Oriental world. Subjects are thus caught in the substantiality of nature, in which they are immersed, although they feel their fundamental differences. Therefore, Asia essentially shows the dawn of the spirit. Hegel says: "At this stage, the state is already present, but the subject has not yet come into its right. Ethical life has an immediate and lawless character, for this is the childhood of history" (198).

In the World of Greece, social differentiations appear. Individuals are more and more conscious but they are at an elementary level in their exigency of freedom. Being finite, they discover their subjective and essential infinity but still in-itself. Such a differentiation has not reached a stage that is advanced enough to allow a global possession of individuals and their proper beings. Hegel says: "The principle of individuality, of subjective freedom, has its origin here, although it is still embedded in the substantial unity" (202).

Thus, the individual specification happens in a form of a societal split into heterogeneous groups that do not yet consciously perceive their universal spirituality through their individual particularities. Individuals discover their perfectibility in themselves and in relation to a being ideally considered Absolute. Society's universal spirituality reveals itself to them in the form of that ideally perfect being. They perceive themselves as the docile subjects of that being they consider transcendent and supreme. There is an assumed split between the human and the divine. At the same time, they develop a self-consciousness of a submission to this divine being in order to realize themselves as perfect beings.

This situation leads to a necessary union between humans and the divine. Humans have not yet uncovered the fact that the divine is not an external reality. They themselves are part of that divine, which is nothing than the Absolute spirit in development. This process of human alienation from their proper essence—and the world essence—conceived as external and transcendent, represents a stage of self-objectification of the Absolute spirit that human beings present as transcendence. This passive submission prevents human beings from discovering the real path to their promotion from servile labor, proper to slaves who are not considered human. Reduced to bestial activity, labor at this precise stage of individual self-consciousness has not yet reached the status of an essential mean for human beings to realize themselves in the actualization of the Absolute spirit.

The differentiation in relation to nature and to global society has not yet engendered an antagonistic character, profound enough to determine the necessity of mastering nature among human beings: it is simply arbitrary. With the rise of numerous states in Greece, there is a simple ethical order, which tends to stand opposite the finite and the infinite, the perfectible and the idealized perfect. In so doing, this ethical life will reveal itself as a supreme contradiction that will be transcended only in the Roman empire.

In the Roman World individuals are fully conscious of their universality, ending thus the process of social differentiation and the multitude of arbitrary states in the Greek world. This process is broken up to form one unique state with its laws and constitutions that individuals must obey. This is determined by the fact that individuals, in the consciousness of their particular subjective universality, cannot individually bring that universality to term. Indeed, all individuals, carrying in themselves that universality, actualize it only in the form of a total seizure of everything that represents the universal. A contradiction then arises between the individual universality still for itself, and therefore abstract in its realization, and the social universality, i.e. the universality of all individuals in their totality. This contradiction is the supreme split between the individual and the social, the particular and the general. It is then only transcended in the form of a state, which through the creation of laws and institutions presents itself as the objective mean of concretizing the subjective and abstract universality. The concrete universal, *de facto* and *de jure,* establishes individual private property. It goes without saying that such a private property, in its intrinsic particularity, is not sufficient for individuals as universal beings. Individuals, through the primacy given to the personality by history, can no longer be self-sufficient.

However, the state, stemming from all the particular individualities, compels humans to be so, and that is why they cannot entirely fulfill a single individual universality. In the long run, the state eventually oppresses the universal subjective and only exercises its authority and power on the individual will in the form of a dictate and arbitrary violence. The rational power of the state is only perceived as an oppressive power against which individuals in their singularities are helpless. Therefore, they surrender to the state but only externally. In reality, the pressing aspiration to the universal, which animates them and which is necessarily limited and confined at the state level, does not and cannot in any way lose power, for it simply internalizes itself. Hegel says: "Thus, an arbitrary power comes into play, reconciling the antithesis and establishing order and peace. But this peace is accompanied by absolute internal disunion; the reconciliation of the anti-thesis is purely worldly and external in character, and it is accordingly counterbalanced by internal insurgency as the pains of despotism make themselves felt" (205).

Thus, the Absolute internal tear of the universal subjective individual stands opposite the apparent peace that reigns between the individual and the state. In this climate of apparent peace and quiet, the individual's absolute but sound refusal—because it is internalized as a free consciousness—echoes the absolute and impersonal power of the state authority. This second and supreme contradiction can no longer be resolved except in the confinement of a tormented life of inwardness in which the spirit progressively begins to discover itself in its perfect immediacy.

It is among the German nations that the spirit discovers itself as fully self-sufficient through individuals that retreated into in themselves and are beyond the stage of a simple mastery of nature. The spirit then will surpass the external contradiction with the universal state to establish the contemplation of its proper self as a goal, which puts an end to the infinite tear in the ethical life.

In the Germanic World, the concrete universal—the state—can in no way satisfy the sphere of individual exigencies, which is the expression of the universal but in a form that is still abstract. At this superior stage, the state has already contained and limited individuals, enough for them to withdraw into themselves and to delight in observing their inner lives and profound subjectivities. This subjective withdrawal and observation of oneself as spirituality progressively led individuals to discover their own nature—which is the expression of the Absolute spirit that reaches the consciousness of itself and contemplates itself in all its plenitude. What was only potentiality in-itself and latency becomes a perfect totality because it is conscious of its perfection. One must understand here that the direct perception of subjectivity, and therefore of the full consciousness of oneself without any intermediary, forms the basis on which the spirit, in revealing itself in its entire splendor, sets itself up as Absolute. Hegel says: "The empire of self-knowing subjectivity marks the rise of the real spirit; this is the beginning of the fourth phase in history, which, in natural terms, would correspond to the old age of the spirit" (205).

The internal and contradictory split, which used to characterize the spirit, disappears and "the spirit as infinite power contains within itself moments of its earlier development and thereby attains its totality" (205-6). Nevertheless, we have only reached the initial phase of the ultimate moment in the spirit odyssey. The self-contemplation of its own subjectivity certainly leads the spirit to perceive itself as a perfection of being but still in an abstract manner. By only having a self-to-self relation, the spirit remains an abstraction in relation to the profane and secular world that is abandoned in a dull contingency. Islam best characterizes this situation of the spirit in its perfect abstraction, and its truth is still hovering over the world. Indeed, everywhere, Islam has proclaimed the uniqueness of God, thereby revealing to humans the universal spirit as being one and indivisible. However, it was just a beginning, therefore an announcement to the world of the incarnation of the spirit becoming world spirit, and thereby set itself up as the real spirit, concrete freedom, and universality.

This situation can be described as the Christian Germanic world, in which individuals become for themselves concrete universals and find that their full realization equals a total appropriateness to the universal. Through Christ, the absolute spirit descends on earth beyond their initial opposition. Then the Christianized world becomes the spirit's ground of incarnation, meaning the disappearance of the natural and subjective arbitrary from this world. At the same time, the spirit also takes the form of the profane while remaining Absolute. This connection between spirit and world, Church and state, progressively leads us to the end of history with the realization of the spirit's goal. Hegel says: "It is this triumphant progress that gives history its interest, and the point at which reconciliation and existence for itself are reached is now an object of knowledge: reality is transformed and reconstructed. This is the goal of world history: the spirit must create for itself a nature and world to conform to its own nature" (208). Thus the only thing left for the universal and concrete spirit is to increase its already eternal perfection for itself.

Africa, the Unhistorical Society

We have just described the principles and progressive stages of historical societies from a Hegelian perspective. Where does Africa fit in all this? Does it have states, political and military movements, in short, a history? Hegel's answer is clear: Africa has no history no matter how active its scene is. It may have had great empires, nevertheless it is a society located out of the historical field.

If Hegel has not included Africa in the determination of historical process in human societies, it is precisely because he does not credit the continent with any history in the sense that he understands the concept. In its process of liberation, the Absolute spirit has not emerged in Africa. However, that does not in anyway mean a total absence of that spirit in Africans. It just exists in the form of a total self-unconsciousness. Africans simply remain people of nature at a primitive stage because "the natural spirit" animates them. Thus, Africa is only the sphere of the unconscious spirit, its direct and massive identification and participation in the almighty nature, which is indeed fundamentally decisive. That is why in African societies, no state, religious, judicial, martial, and artistic activity can be oriented toward the realization of an ideal or ethic.

Africans, more precisely Negroes, are people solely dominated by preoccupations that are purely carnal and biological. Africans are not aware of their human status. They just perceive themselves as being carnal and natural and therefore, they miss their potential humanity. Hegel says: "Thus man as we have found him in Africa has not progressed beyond his immediate existence. As soon as man emerges as a human being, he stands in opposition to nature, and it is this alone that makes him a human being. But if he has merely made a distinction himself and nature, he is still at the first stage of his development: he is dominated by passion, and is nothing more than a savage" (177).

It is thus precisely because of their latent humanity that Africans can distinguish themselves from nature, but in so far as that humanity remains forever in this state of itself. Africans remain incapable of objectifying nature and perceive it as something external in-itself and are unable to oppose it. On the contrary, such distinction remains formal, and throughout the Negro activities, a savage and brutal naturalness—escaping from all real morality—appears. To the total lack of ideal among Negroes one can add the quasi-total lack of ethic and religious sense. Such an almost absolute domination of the biological defines the social forms as many means for the amoral Negroes to obtain pleasure, and this, at any cost. Hegel says:

> From all these various traits we have enumerated, it can be seen that intractability is the distinguishing feature of the Negro character. The condition in which they live is incapable of any development or culture, and their present existence is the same as it has always been. In face of the enormous energy of sensuous arbitrariness, which dominates their lives, morality has no determinate influence upon them. Anyone who wishes to study the most terrible manifestations of human nature will find them in Africa. (190)

The humanity Hegel mentions here is just formal. Africans are like spoilt children who, in the warmth of the unconsciousness of their maternal womb, only perceive themselves as a body of biological needs to satisfy. After being born, they can only see themselves as individualities restricted to an instinct of self-preservation, and this independently of any morale, which, by the way, they do not recognize, and are unable to know. We could think that the love that such children feel for their mothers could show that there are human feelings in them, but that is far from being the case. That love is physical in its content as well as in its goal. The childlike humanity remains potential because not yet conscious, spiritual, or oriented to moral goals. Negroes can be understood as such. Everything in them only prefigures the human without ever being so. They reduce everything to their desires and passions, and this with a characteristic innocence. The external world, law, and God are unconsciously assimilated to their properly biological selves as many means of satisfying their natural needs. That is why in the end Hegel says:

> The Negro is an example of animal man in all his savagery and lawlessness, and if we wish to understand him at all, we must put aside all our European attitudes. We must not think of a spiritual God or of moral laws; to comprehend him correctly, we must abstract from all reverence and morality, and from everything which we call feeling. All this is foreign to man in his immediate existence, and nothing consonant with humanity is to be found in his character. (177)

That is why in no matter what field of activity, one cannot but notice in Negroes this biological inhumanity, which veils, if not dissolves, almost integrally a humanity that is simply ideal but not really present. Can we at this point talk about Hegel's unequal considerations of nations? Would Africans or Negroes simply be inferior regarding other nations and races? It seems that the answer is no and that Hegel is much more radical towards Africans. There is a qualitative difference between historical and unhistorical societies, but there is a neat qualitative difference between African species and the other historical people. Negro Africans certainly represent a complicated enough level of quantitative and biological complexity, which allows them to distinguish themselves from a pure bestiality. They are right between a quantitatively superior bestiality and a humanity that has not begun. In their different social activities, such a pre-human character neatly reveals itself.

Religion, Witchcraft, and the Cult of the Dead

Let us mention first that for Hegel, religion, before anything else consists of human beings' objectification and recognition of a superior power. The true religion thus, is the one in which the power in question is of spiritual nature. The fact of believing in natural forces such as the sun, stars, water, etc., does indicate a religious attitude, which is however less manifest and therefore inferior. Religion, although being the most general form of human alienation—in the sense that it accepts a superior power such as God—is nevertheless a superior stage of human self-consciousness and therefore, of evolution. However, human beings do not recognize their essential unity with the divine or they only do so in the form of a submission to that divine. Any other process in this historically determined phase would only be a caricature or an absence of religion. Yet at this precise level, Africans' attitude becomes one of the most original. Hegel says: "The character of the Africans shows the antithesis between man and nature in its earliest form. In this condition, man sees himself and nature as opposed to one another, but with himself in the commanding position; this is the basic situation in Africa" (179).

In other words, Africans do not only recognize a superior, natural, or spiritual element, but they also consider themselves superior elements capable of influencing nature. They obey the infantile feeling of the almighty self. They reduce everything to themselves and believe they are capable of everything. But this compatibility exists only in an illusory and arbitrary form. Africans do not talk about an effective mastery of nature by technical and directly productive activities. In Hegel's words: "The Negroes' consciousness of nature is not a consciousness of its objective existence; still less is it a consciousness of God as a spirit, as something higher in and for itself than nature. Nor do they possess that understanding that uses nature as a means—by sailing on the sea, for example, and generally exercising control over nature. The Negroes' power over nature is only an imaginary power, an illusory authority" (182).

Africans only content themselves by giving orders to nature and being obeyed. They only see in front of themselves a nature they recognize as the ensemble of natural forces and nothing more. Hegel says: "But although these natural forces, as well as sun, moon, trees, and animals, are recognized as powers in their own rights, they are not seen as having an eternal law or providence behind them, or as forming parts of a universal and permanent natural order" (179).

Self-intuition as different from nature creates in Africans the illusion that they can subdue nature with the instrument of that very intuition, which is a rather natural spirituality in terms of its content. That is why here we must talk about a magical attitude or sorcery among Africans and give reason to Herodotus for whom "all Africans are sorcerers" (179). Indeed in sorcery people consider themselves Gods with occult powers capable of warding off natural dangers and drawing benefits for themselves. All this is done by way of libations and incantations, which only draw their strength and impact from sorcerers themselves.

Is this a form of atheism? Most likely not. Here God is not recognized, but with the unique mode of subjectivity falsely full of itself, Africans illusively take God's place. In the rational essence of atheism, god is not discarded for the pleasure of doing so, but is explained and understood as an irrational product of alienated reason. Africans' non-recognition of God is close to an animal's unconsciousness of any divinity. Even if Africans happen to use fetishes in their magical and ritual practices, it does in no way mean that they grant those fetishes any superior power as a possible mediation between humans and the divine. The fetishes are not considered an incarnation of God or any superior power. Thus, there is no totemism or idolatry here for us to talk about a true religion of nature, which nevertheless represents the lowest relationship humans can entertain with a God in a natural spirituality. Sorcery in Africa is below a barely elaborated level. The choice of fetish among Africans is undifferentiated. Their interest is to show and represent their own power through any natural material, which in any case remains secondary. Hegel says: "The second feature of their religion is that they give this power of theirs a visible form, projecting it out of their own consciousness and making images of it. The first object that they encounter, which they imagine has power over them—whether it be an animal, a tree, or a wooden image—is given the status of a genius" (180). The fetish is thus purely artificial, without any metaphysical consistency, and the user can reject or destroy it at any given moment. Hegel says:

> In the fetish, the arbitrary will of the individual does seem to be faced with an independent entity, but since the object in question is nothing more than the will of the individual projected into a visible form, this will in fact remains master of the image it has adopted. What they regard as their ruling power is therefore not an objective entity with an independent existence distinct from their own. The fetish remains in their power, and they reject it when it does not

do their will. They then adopt something else as their higher authority and imagine that it exercises power over them, but keep it in their own power for this very reason. If something unpleasant occurs, which the fetish has failed to avert, the oracles that they have consulted are deemed to be false and become discredited. If the rain does not come or the crops do badly, they bind and beat the fetish or destroy and discard it, and at once create another to take its place. In other words, their God remains in their power, to be acknowledged and rejected at will, so that they do not progress beyond a condition of arbitrariness. (180-1)

However, not everyone possesses this privilege. This magical power is concentrated in the hands of only a few individuals. They use it for the benefit of their king, armies, and their countries. If heir commands prove persistently ineffectual, they are severely punished. Sometimes, these sorcerers order human sacrifices of their own dearest relatives, which of course is a proof of an indifferent inhumanity. Hegel says: "In practice, therefore, only some individuals have power over nature, and these only when they are beside themselves in a state of dreadful enthusiasm" (180). This state allows them to elevate themselves above the others and to command the elements as mediators between nature and society. The same behavior toward fetishes—with a slight difference—is found in the African cult of the dead, with the only difference Hegel mentions: "And it is the same with the spirit of the dead, to whom they attribute a mediating function like that of the sorcerers. These spirits are also men, but what does suggest the presence of a higher authority here is that they are men who have cast off their immediate existence" (181). And the dead are capable of reacting to the solicitations or attacks from the living.

Let us not forget that among Africans death is not considered a natural phenomenon, but rather the tragic result of a fate or spell an enemy has cast. Therefore, the dead are endowed with hostile intentions. And it is precisely to ward off such intentions that individuals organize sacrifices or recite incantations in order to gain and, if possible, obtain their good will. Hegel says: "Their deceased ancestors and forefathers are regarded as a power capable of acting against the living. They resort to these spirits in the same way as to fetishes, offering them sacrifices and conjuring them up; but where this proves unsuccessful, they punish the departed ancestor himself, casting his bones away and desecrating his remains" (181). This is as if the departed should satisfy the living's whims. Nevertheless, in the Negro mentality, the dead react and are mostly responsible for societal ailments. One could think that, because they are out of their immediate existence, the dead constitute a qualitatively superior order for Africans. It is quite the contrary. In fact, they maintain a relationship of interdependence with society and not a unilateral adoration from the living. Hegel says: "The African knows nothing of what we call the immortality of the soul. They do recognize what we call ghost, but this is not the same thing as immortality: for immortality implies that man is a spiritual being in and for himself, and that his nature is unchanging and eternal" (182).

In their incapacity of conceiving a spiritual order, Negroes bathe in simple naturalness and can never recognize a spiritual and objective eternity that is transcendental and inherent to death. So do they only prefigure the dawn of the religious spirit with their powerless and inefficient figurines. In short, Africans do not have a religion per se because they are located out of the universal spirit's most elementary moment of objectivity.

Customs and State

Negro manners and customs are among the strangest ones. They have special characteristics, radically different from the other races' and nations', as Hegel explains:

> This character, however, is difficult to comprehend, because it is so totally different from our own culture, and so remote and alien in relation to our own mode of consciousness. We must forget all the categories that are fundamental to our own spiritual life, i.e. the forms under which we normally subsume the data that confront us; the difficulty here is that our customary preconceptions will still inevitably intrude in all our deliberations. (176)

We guess that here Hegel suspects a certain potential Eurocentrism that can come from researchers or students of Africa who project their own culture onto the African temperament. Is it truly a prevention of Eurocentrism or its consolidation? It is most likely the latter. If Hegel prevents a projection of European categories onto Africa, it is in the sense of a radical dissociation, therefore a qualitative and essential differentiation between the two societies. Europe, the true center of civilization, cannot lower itself by indentifying with uncivilized and unhistorical Africa. Therefore, one must isolate Africa as much as possible and study it with new lenses as strange as the object of study itself. One can thus expect to see in Africa any bizarre form of manifestation that would be incomprehensible, if not negatively out of the ordinary.

Thus Africans represent the pre-human order. In such a case, how can they have any kind of respect for humans, the superior order and value, and thus for themselves? By virtue of their superiority, humans respect and valorize others through themselves. However, Africans lack that quality. Therefore, Negroes can only deprecate their kind: "The Negroes have, therefore, a complete *contempt* for man, and it is this above all that determines their attitude towards justice and morality. Their belief in the worthlessness of man goes to almost incredible lengths; their political order can be regarded as tyranny, but this is considered perfectly legitimate and is not felt to constitute an injustice" (182).

We can be tempted to believe that Negroes' great courage, which leads them to defend themselves when they need to, is a proof that they have a certain valorization of themselves through a moral ideal and a will of independence. Far from it. Such courage has no determined orientation in the sense of their self-preservation or liberation. Negroes are essentially exuberant and their actions have no finality if not in an unjustified violence for violence's sake. Only a superficial spirit can consider such an attitude a true courage in the sense that courage implies a spiritual consciousness of its value i.e. the necessity of self-protection. There is no need to pretend to find out whether such a value really exists among Negroes. What about Negroes' bloody revolts against servitude or foreign domination? Hegel explains: "In the war between the Ashanti and the English, the natives persisted in running straight up to the mouth of the cannon although they were invariably shot down fifty at a time. In fact, life is of no value unless it has a worthy object" (185).

All this, thus is determined by a profound contempt for life and a constitutive physical fanaticism. Life does not disgust Negroes. They are not and the existential feeling of the absurdity of human life cannot haunt them. Only a superior consciousness in the human order can detect such absurdity of life. It reveals a radical opposition between human spiritual aspiration and a totally hostile nature. This depreciation of life among Negroes once more belongs to the pre-human order; that is why they are inclined to death as well as to life. Indeed, if life has no value, it rightfully equals death and that is why to kill or to be killed means nothing to Negroes. It would then be inconsequent to notice any such thing as love of life in the Negroes' apparent courageous behavior.

Any cause, even of the slightest importance, unleashes the Negro's murderous madness. That cause is perceived as something supreme that offers a ground for the justification of all sorts of atrocities. The supremacy of the cause—which can be extremely futile—is due to the fact that: "The realm of the spirit is so poor among them, and yet the spirit itself is so intensive that any idea that is disseminated among them may drive them to respect nothing and destroy everything" (188). The tiniest breach of the spirit still in itself suffices to make their organism accomplish the unconceivable things. Negroes are then like fanatics but of a more physical than spiritual fanaticism. The destructive flash of thought, which appears in their extremely elementary mind, only instills a unilateral orientation into their impulses. Africans' fanaticism thus does not have a real spiritual foundation. It shows itself through an unleashing of vile and destructive instincts. Whom to destroy? Anybody. It includes people who belong to their own societies.

Hegel, referring to an English traveler's report, says: "When the Ashanti have resolved to go to war, solemn ceremonies are first enacted; these include the washing of the bones of the king's mother with human blood. As a preliminary to war, the king decrees an attack on his own capital, in order to drive himself into a fury" (188). And then, "The drum was sounded; the warriors of the king, armed with short swords, went out on their murderous mission, and a terrible bloodbath ensued; all who encountered the frenzied Negroes as they rushed through the streets were struck down" (188). When the king dies, it turns into a massacre that can only be stopped with the proclamation of a new king. When impulses—the determining flash in their natural thought—has disappeared. Negroes suddenly calm down and enter into the gloomy tranquility of a life with no spiritual value at all.

Anthropophagy, among other traits, is one of the fundamental characteristics of African customs, and its foundation unquestionably remains in the total contempt Africans feel towards humans. Hegel says: "All men who have progressed even to a limited degree in consciousness have respect for human beings as such" (183). It is precisely this little progress that is lacking among Africans. That is why they essentially consider themselves being of flesh and bones and nothing else. However, humans are not a simple biological complex limited to a simple naturalness; they are able to think and therefore possess a soul, which is the foundation of that very thought. There is no such thing in the Negro conception. Hegel says: "To the sensuous Negro, human flesh is purely an object of the senses, like all other flesh" (183). That is why Negroes do not hesitate to eat it. Hegel says: "The eating of human flesh is quite compatible with the African principle" (183). Not only is this anthropophagy a current practice, but it is also institutionalized according to Hegel. Moreover, the custom requires that during festivities prisoners' heads be offered as food to their victors. Negroes even sell human flesh at the market, says Hegel. This practice has become a way of life that Africans do not condemn at all.

It goes without saying that this unique contempt for human beings does not end with these two aspects. Negroes also advocate and do practice slavery among and against themselves. Hegel says that in Africa, "the basic principle of all slavery is that man is not yet conscious of his freedom, and consequently sinks to the level of a mere object or worthless article" (183). Yet, Negroes still carry in themselves the seed of their own surpassing. The slave condition, to which they are compelled, makes them aware of their self-conscious being. They then experience slavery as a supreme alienation, which their consciousness at first and secretly revolts against. This inner revolt matures their spirit in the sense of their universal or their concrete liberation. If by its very content slavery is thus something negative, it develops in human beings a process of negativity that leads to freedom. It arises as a negative process of human self-liberation and disappears with the rational state, the expression of human freedom.

This dialectical process is absent in the Negroes. The idea of a revolt does not cross their minds, even if they are in a state of servitude. On the contrary, they take pleasure in it and find it normal. Therefore, they do not challenge the slave condition to which the Europeans have reduced them. They go as far as to blame and treat their saviors as enemies. Hegel says: "The Negroes see nothing improper about it [slavery], and the English, although they have done the most to abolish slavery and the slave trade, are treated as enemies by the Negroes themselves" (183).

The only potentially positive aspect of this slavery is the remote possibilities for a European civilization to embrace Negroes. As for the relationships among themselves in terms of slavery, Negroes are of a complete inhumanity. Kings sell their prisoners as well as their own subjects. They collect women to produce many kids to be sold. Hegel says: "The polygamy of the Negroes often has the sole object of producing many children, so that they can all be sold as slaves; they are quite oblivious of the injustice of this situation. Indeed, they carry this anomaly to unbound lengths. The king of Dahomey, for example, has 3,333 wives; every rich man has various, and his many children provide him with a new source of revenue" (185). Slavery thus explains polygamy in Africa. Negroes do not have a multitude of wives because they love them; they are just means to procreate and sell children. They even, if need be, sell their whole family since family as defined does not involve any sentimental or ethical relation. All this happens in a total lack of scruples or moral prejudices.

There is finally the African state, which has no constitution and is founded on the arbitrary rule of a despot. A constitution defines a set of principles aiming at regulating social life. These principles stem from the conscious and rational popular will, which confers it a legal status, juridically valid for everybody. Such is the foundation of the constitutional state, representative of the universal spirit. And such a state does not exist and cannot exist among Negroes. What we could call state among them can only be in the form of a despotism exercised from the outside. Hegel says: "Where the arbitrary will prevails, there can be no union except that created by external force" (186). The arbitrariness of the natural spirit, dominant among Africans, makes it impossible for a will to unite and emerge from such relationships. The infantile feeling of the almighty self leads particular individuals to seek only his or her own satisfaction. This external force is caused by the fact that a particular free will arises above the arbitrary common will, imposing itself, and thereby compelling cohesion.

The despot's power is not rational and is not founded on a particular individual's consciousness of a spiritual universality as in the case of despotism in historical societies. The unique foundation of such despotism is the desire for an arbitrary will to impose itself onto all others and to direct them toward its interests. This despotism is based on arbitrariness. Nevertheless, it does manifest a despot's superiority in the sense that his or her free will—being above the strict limit of individual particularities—is directed to all individuals and thereby elevate itself above them.

However, despots never perceive themselves as incarnations of any spiritual value, which, in relation to the universal spirit, renders their powers simply formal. From this point of view, the African state is nothing but a caricature. It is an abstract copy of the true state, which in the despotic, spiritual, and constitutional singularity remains the expression of the spirit in development. It thus remains a natural, arbitrary substantiality. That is why the despot's violence is never exclusively efficient; it is in fact limited by the violence of the subjects who, if need be, kill the king. And only subjects powerful enough to oppose the despot can exert such a limitation. That is why, if they don't kill each other, they reach a compromise by which despotism exercises itself in the form of a hierarchical structure.

At the top sits a despot king, underneath him are the chiefs, then the notables, and then the generals with whom he makes common decisions. The despot enjoys a great deal of privilege and can be assassinated if he is unsatisfactory. In short, the attitude toward the sovereign varies a lot depending on the undifferentiated multitude of powerful Negro states; and despotism in general does not have that absolute character that is found elsewhere. Hegel gives an example: "In East Africa, Bruce traveled through a state in which the prime minister was the executioner, although the only person he was permitted to decapitate was the king: thus the sword really hangs above the despot's head day and night" (187). In return and in certain occasions, such as in battles, the despot can order an unlimited continuation of hostilities because at this level he has the worthless lives of his subjects at his disposal. Therefore, one can say that in general despotism in Africa is based on the sovereign's violence as well as on the subjects'. It is thus the definition of a state, not really organized and constantly subject to fluctuations that signals the predominance of natural arbitrariness.

From all these findings about African customs and institutions, Hegel naturally draws the conclusion that Africa is unhistorical. Indeed, where natural spirit—still totally unconscious of its essential universality—absolutely rules, there can be no history, in so far as history is essentially the dialectic and evolutionary process of the spirit's self-consciousness against nature and independently from it. In such a particular context, there can be no historical goal of actualizing individuals that are not yet aware of their humanity, *a fortiori* their spiritual universality. What really characterizes Africa is that history is out of the question. Hegel says: "Life there consists of a succession of contingent happenings and surprises. No aim or state exists whose development could be followed; and there is no subjectivity, but merely a series of subjects who destroy one another" (176).

Africa is steeped in an inessential, amorphous, and static natural materiality, with consciousness here being extremely secondary and totally trapped in nature. Hegel explains: "From the earliest historical times, Africa has remained cut off from all contacts with the rest of the world: It is the land of gold, for ever pressing in upon itself, and the land of childhood, removed from the light of self-conscious history and wrapped in the dark mantle of night" (174). This night of unconsciousness that characterizes the African spirit plunges the continent into a continuous agitation with no conscious finality. After all, Hegel says, "Africa is an unhistorical continent, with no movement or development of its own. What we understand as Africa proper is that unhistorical and underdeveloped land, which is still enmeshed in the natural spirit, and which had to be mentioned here before we cross the threshold of world history itself" (190).

What about Egypt and the northern regions of Africa? They are not part of Africa. Hegel says: "Egypt will be considered as a stage in the movement of the human spirit from east to west, but it has no part in the spirit of Africa" (190). As for northern Africa, its extreme opening to and dependence on the external world must be considered as being out of Africa proper.

Can this unhistorical Africa at least begin a process of evolution in the course of history? In other words, is this unhistoricity simply contingent or structural? Hegel's answer is categorical. If Africa is at the threshold of history, it still is incapable of crossing that threshold. It remains trapped in that sphere with no way out. Hegel says that not only do Africans live in a total and passive autarchy but also "The condition in which they live is incapable of any development or culture, and their present existence is the same as it has always been" (190). Thus, Africa remains static forever. Nevertheless, even from Hegel's perspective, such a severe judgment needs to be tempered. He now considers the possibility for Negroes to gain access to civilization, meaning European civilization. First, he sees in Islam "the only thing that has brought the Negroes at all nearer to culture" (177).

For now, let us simply understand that for Hegel, Africa can only progress thanks to the influence of external factors mostly of European origin. Africa, so to speak, does not have any internal dynamism by which it would make its own history. It can only lag behind qualitatively superior historical societies. And European societies are the culminant point representing the incarnation of the Absolute spirit that has reached a total perfection of itself.

African Hegelianism

In his *Introduction to Africana Philosophy* (2008), Lewis Gordon notes that elements of Hegelian dialectic can be found in the works and thought processes of prominent historical Black thinkers in both North America and the Caribbean. W. E. B. Dubois may have a somewhat different approach to history than Hegel, yet he still uses a dialectic approach to explain the notion of "double consciousness" in his *Black Reconstruction in America* (1935). Gordon mentions other scholars such as Anténor Firmin, C. L. R. James, Aimé Césaire, and Frantz Fanon who also have elements of Kant, Hegel, Marx, and Sartre in their works. John Dewey, whom Cornell West claims to have inspired his philosophy of prophetic pragmatism, has incorporated some Hegelian elements into his work by putting "focus on individuals in community and the dynamic potential of dialectical inquiry" (94).

Gordon deplores the irony in this influence because of Hegel's degrading description of Africa and Africans. He explains: "By virtue of his [Hegel's] claim, history did not even pay a courtesy to visit Black peoples of Africa. Even the virtue of religiosity should not be ascribed to African" (197). Africa is seen as being too barbaric to have a history and therefore it has no place in Hegel's "unfolding realization of reason." Thus, for Gordon, Hegel's' condescending description of Africa was amongst the first in a long history of keeping African philosophy and intellectualism marginalized. Moreover, this notion of Africa being incapable of producing a meaningful and relevant history has left a lasting impression on academia. Consequently, much of African medieval thought and intellectualism has been ignored until fairly recently, in the mid 1900s.

However, this ironic influence reaches a new dimension with Senghor. Many of the early Black intellectuals who set out to oppose Hegel got too close to his theses and ended up revealing similarities with Hegel's position. Senghor's *Negritude*, for example, offers a general theory of the Negro and is meant to advocate the defense of Negro values of civilization. Paradoxically, his view presents striking similarities with Hegelian theses, despite the claim of a neat opposition. Such a situation places intellectuals in what Dieng calls "African Hegelianism."

Senghor and Gobineau's Symbolism

The association of Negroes with an easy inclination to suicide and with the total and consequent lack of value placed on their own lives and human life in general—encountered in the Hegelian thesis—is found in Joseph Arthur Comte de Gobineau (1967): "The negro is equally careless of his own life and that of others: he kills willingly, for the sake of killing; and this human machine, in whom it is so easy to arouse emotion, shows, in the face of suffering, either a monstrous indifference or a cowardice that seeks a voluntary refuge in death" (206).

Sandra Bonetto (2006) criticizes Karl Popper's and Robert Bernasconi's linking of Hegel's name with that of racist ideologues, such as Robert Knox and the very Gobineau just mentioned, who are often seen as precursors of fascism or modern racism. Her conclusion exonerates Hegel. However, it becomes quite stunning to find Senghor's thesis expressed in almost the same terms, in the first edition of Le Comte de Gobineau's *Essay* (1967), even if Gobineau's language is cruder and his arguments are more grotesque. Describing the Negro, Gobineau says:

> The negroid variety is the lowest and stands at the foot of the ladder. The animal character that appears in the shape of the pelvis is stamped on the negro from birth, and foreshadows his destiny. His intellect will always move within a very narrow circle. He is not however a mere brute, for behind his low receding brow, in the middle of his skull, we can see signs of a powerful energy, however crude its objects. If his mental faculties are dull or even non-existent, he often has an intensity of desire, and so of will, which may be called terrible (205).

For Gobineau, Negroes' sensations are not only intense but also impulsive, and therein lies their inferiority. Many of the Negro senses, especially taste and smell, are developed to an extent unknown to the other two races—European and Asian. So great is Negroes' gift of sensuality that they would be entirely submissive to external excitations. That is why:

All food is good in his eyes. Nothing disgusts or repels him. What he desires to eat he eats furiously and to excess; no carrion is too revolting to be swallowed by him. It is the same with odors; his inordinate desires are satisfied with [everything], however coarse or even horrible. We might even say that the violence with which he pursues the object that has aroused his senses and inflamed his desires is a guarantee of the desires being soon satisfied and the object forgotten (205-06).

These theses, presenting Africa as the domain of the sensual and the empiric, are also found in Senghor in a slightly modified form. The theorist of *Négritude* explains, "Le nègre ne sait ni diviser ni compter, pas même distinguer" [Negroes do not know how to divide or count, or even differentiate] (100). Before Senghor, Gobineau also believes that the exposition of an algebra problem leaves Negroes cold. For Senghor, the racial psychic division provides Whites with the sense of reasoning that gave birth to the sciences. As for Negroes, they are the proprietors of sensuality and emotionality from which artistic genius springs. For Gobineau (1853), "Le nègre est la création la plus énergiquement saisie par la création artistique" [Negroes' irresistible attraction toward artistic creation] (360).

For Senghor, the Negro soul is unstable because of inconstant external excitations affecting it. The immediacy and the overlapping of the Negro's reactions create a perpetual fluctuation of emotions. They continually jump from one state to another and from one humor to another, driven by emotions created by external causes. With Negroes, all states of mind are transitory, unexpected and contradictory. But well before Senghor, Gobineau (1856) had developed the same opinion: "To these traits, he [the Negro] joins a childish instability of humor. His feelings are intense, but not enduring. His grief is as transitory as it is poignant, and he rapidly passes from it to extreme gayety. He is seldom vindictive—his anger is violent, but soon dissipated" (445). Previously he noted that Negroes add to their character "an instability and capriciousness of feeling that cannot be tied down to any single object" (215).

There are definitely similarities between Gobineau's theses and Senghor's on the Negro's psychological faculties. Senghor obviously has read Gobineau since he quotes him in his writings. As for Whites, Senghor affirms that they are sensually less gifted than Negroes: "In the world of the senses, the white man is far less gifted" (207). However, this inferiority in Whites goes with an incontestable superiority in the domain of the spirit. He notes: "The immense superiority of the white peoples in the whole field of the intellect is balanced by an inferiority in the intensity of their sensations" (207). Inversely, the hypertrophic sensuality of Negroes is commensurate with the nullity of their intellect, which, according to him, is incapable "de s'élever au-dessus du plus humble niveau du mouvement qu'il faut pour réfléchir, apprendre, comparer, tirer des conséquences" [of rising above the most basic level of the inclination necessary to think, learn, compare, and draw conclusions] (360). More than a century later,

Senghor (1984) claims: "L'émotion est nègre comme la raison est hellène" [Emotion is Negro, reason is Greek] (24): Whites think and Negroes feel; Whites have more mind than Negroes but Negroes have more soul than Whites.

Negro Mysticism and Lucien Levy-Bruhl

According to Senghor, Negroes have very developed senses. They feel the world through their pores and perceive the smallest vibration of objects. In Kantian terms, they do not limit themselves to the material and phenomenal universe. Rather, they transcend it to seize the essence, which is the profound and invisible true being. While White people limit themselves to the ostensible and superficial, Negroes seize the fundamental reality beyond its outward appearance. That, according to Senghor, is indubitably spirit. In such a perspective, the object is not isolated or detached from the idea, nor is it a shadow, a copy, or a projection of the idea either: the object is the spirit's external envelope, its place of habitation. That is why Senghor affirms that for Negroes "Sous l'aspect matériel et sensible, il y a un monde d'âmes" [Beneath the material and sensitive world, there is world of souls] (71).

Before Senghor, Levy-Bruhl developed the same idea at length: "In all forms of being, and behind all natural phenomena, they imagine 'soul,' 'spirits,' 'intentions,' similar to those they believe they have experienced in themselves and their companions, and in animals" (19). Thus, Levy-Bruhl's idealism of the primitive and Senghor's Negro postulate the immanence of one or several spirits inside a matter that they animate. Senghor notes: "On peut dire que c'est une forme spirituelle, un principe de vie intellectuelle et morale qui anime chaque être, chaque plante, chaque chose pourvue d'un charactère propre: montagne, caverne, rocher, lac" [We can say that it is a spiritual form, a principle of intellectual and moral life, which animates each human being, plant, things that are endowed with a character proper: mountains, caves, rocks, lakes] (71). As for Levy-Bruhl, he categorically concludes: "But we have to bear in mind that which their collective representations instill into all their perceptions. Whatever object is presented to their minds, it implies mystic properties, which are inextricably bound up with it, and the primitive, in perceiving it, never separates these from it" (43). His logic is based on a certain valorization of Negro emotionality, very similar to Senghor's theory. For Levy-Bruhl, Negroes' perception of the world is inseparable from the emotional tremors around it. And their emotions constitute the basis of their mystical impulses. He notes:

> Whenever the object of one of these representations once more arises in the consciousness of the "primitive," even should he be alone and in a calm frame of mind at the moment, it can never appear to him as a colorless and indifferent image; a wave of emotion will immediately surge over him, undoubtedly less intense than it was during the ceremonies, but yet strong enough for its cognitive aspect to be almost lost sight of in the emotions that surround it. (37)

Therefore, the belief in the supernatural is already inscribed into the primitive mental structure and, more precisely, into its overflowing imagination which results from a great emotivity. Levy-Bruhl notes: "Thus rocks, the form or position of which strike the primitive's imagination, readily assume a sacred character in virtue of their supposed mystic power. Similar power is ascribed to the rivers, clouds, and winds. Districts in space, direction (the points of the compass), have mystic significance" (40). He adds: "If we recall the myths of which animals are the heroes, in both hemispheres, there is no mammal or bird or fish or even insect to which the most extraordinary mystic properties have not been attributed" (39); moreover, "If we consider the human body, we shall find that each organ of it has its own mystic significance" (39). The mysticism of the primitives then rests on a hermeneutic: one must uncover the spirit or soul behind the material envelope of objects. Matter in its diversity functions as an ensemble of signs to be interpreted, of symbols to connect to a profound meaning.

The Senghorian picture of Negro vision is similar to Levy-Bruhl's. In this same order of ideas, Senghor states that, for Negro-Africans, "Chaque appel retentit profondément en lui jusqu'à l'intérieur de ses os" [Each call resounds deeply in him, all the way to his bones] (71). In relation to White people, Negroes have the advantage of seizing all the excitations from the object, but also the mystical gift of discovering its supernatural dimension. Senghor says: "Les nègres sont ouverts à tous les objets, à tous les contacts, à toutes les sollicitations et jusqu'aux moindres soufflés" [Negroes are receptive to all objects, all contacts, all stimulations, and to the slightest wiff] (62-63).

The profound and mystical meaning of the object, thus, is what interests Negroes and provokes their emotional shock. In this sense, Senghor writes: "Ce qui émeut le noir ce n'est pas l'aspect exterieur de l'objet, c'est sa réalité ou mieux, sa surréalité" [What moves the Negro is not the external appearance of the object. It is its reality, or better its surreality] (263). However, the Negro interpretation of the world is not only mystic, but also anthropomorphic. Nature is not endowed with simply any spirit: it is endowed with a *human spirit*. With the help of sensibility and emotion, Negroes have learned to perceive the world and to attribute human thought to it. As Senghor says: "Ainsi toute la nature est animée d'une pensée humaine. Elle s'humanise au sens étymologique et actuel du mot. Non seulement les animaux et les phenomènes de la nature—pluie, vent, tonnere, fleuve—mais encore l'arbre et le caillou se font des hommes. Hommes qui gardent les caractères physiques originaux comme instruments de signes de leur âme personnelle" [All nature is thus animated by human thought. It becomes human in the etymological and real sense of the word. Not only animals and natural phenomena—rain, wind, thunder, river—but also trees and pebbles turn into men. Men who keep their original physical characteristics as instruments of signs of their personal soul] (24-25).

However, according to Senghor, Negroes' cosmogony is not speculative, but practical, and guides them in their attitudes and relations with the universe. Because they see themselves through the universe, Negroes' relations with the natural milieu are full of harmony and sympathy. Their preoccupation is not to dominate nature, but to participate in its life, for the real is a prolongation of their spirits, a duplication of their souls. That is why, according to Senghor, the Negro's reason is not an instrument of world domination or a ruse to appropriate the object, as is the case with White reason. On the contrary, Negro reason is a human means of communication, interjection and participation in the equilibrium of cosmic forces. Senghor writes: "La raison européenne est analytique par utilisation, la raison nègre intuitive par participation" [European reason is analytic and makes use of the object. Negro reason is intuitive through participation] (203).

All the same, this conception is not original. Before Senghor, Levy-Bruhl attributed the same characteristics to the "primitive mentality." For primitives, a mystical relationship unites them to occult realities because they cannot dissociate the object from the soul that is supposed to inhabit it. They are insensitive to contradiction and are only interested in connections—or, rather, pre-associations—in a universe where nothing is isolated. Levy-Bruhl thus goes on: "We have to bear in mind that which their collective representations instill into their perception. Whatever the object presented to their minds, it implies mystic properties, which are inextricably bound up with it, and the primitive, in perceiving it, never separates these from it" (43). Levy-Bruhl illustrates his thesis by quoting Miss Alice Fletcher's comments on the mysticism of North American Indians:

> [They] regarded all animate and inanimate forms, all phenomena as pervaded by a common life, which was continuous and similar to the will power they were conscious of in themselves. This mysterious power in all things they called *Wakonda*, and through it all things were related to man, and to each other. In the idea of the continuity of life, a relation was maintained between the seen and the unseen, the dead and the living, and also between the fragment of anything and its entirety. (103)

Levy-Bruhl adds: "Here continuity means what we call participation, since this continuity obtains between the living and the dead; between a man's nail-parings, saliva, or hair and the man himself: between a certain bear or buffalo and the mystic ensemble of the bear or buffalo species" (132). It is therefore no surprise that such a mentality is not analytical, confuses the subjective with the objective, and does not attach any importance to experimentation and verification. Levy-Bruhl notes:

> Miss Kingsley relates that she once heard a Negro talking aloud, as if conversing with an interlocutor unseen by her. Upon inquiry, she found that the Negro was talking to his dead mother who, according to him, was present. To the primitive, the reality of the objects he perceives does not in the least depend upon his being able to verify this reality by what we call experience; indeed, as a rule, it is the intangible and invisible that is most real in his eyes. (302)

Thus, Levy-Bruhl concludes: "The law of participation governs in despotic fashion the collective representations upon which these practices depend; and permits of the most flagrant contradictions in these" (303). In other words, the ascendancy of the sacred over the primitives' mental activity—which includes Negroes—contributes to the fact that they have not reached the acquisition of a logic that dates back to Aristotle.

Negro Ontology and the Reverend Father Placide Tempels

The first French edition of the missionary Tempels' *La philosophie bantoue* was published in 1945 in the Belgian Congo. By 1949 it had been reprinted three times by the famous African-founded publishing house *Présence Africaine*. The book was so successful among African scholars and most of all, among the Negritude militants, that in the preface of the second edition, the founding editor Alioune Diop wrote: "Voici un livre essentiel au noir, à sa prise de conscience, à sa soif de se situer par rapport à l'Europe. Il doit aussi être le livre de chevet de tous ceux qui se préoccupent de comprendre l'Africain et d'engager un dialogue vivant avec lui" [Here is an essential book for Negroes, their *prise de conscience*, and their thirst to situate themselves in relation to Europe. It should also be a bedside book for all those who are concerned with understanding Africans and engaging in vital dialogue with them] (6). Summarizing an almost general feeling among advocates of Negritude—except maybe for Césaire who virulently criticizes the book—Diop confesses: "Pour moi, ce petit livre est le plus important de ceux que j'ai lus sur l'Afrique. Il contribue à révéler l'âme du Nègre authentique, inséré dans son vivifiant milieu naturel" [To me, this little book is the most important one I have ever read about Africa. It contributes to revealing the soul of the authentic Negro, inserted in his active natural environment] (6).

The book was not only a miraculous weapon for Black intellectuals seeking their specific soul, but it also influenced White supporters such as the ones Senghor often quotes. Dieng (1978) tells us, "Gaston Bachelard et les philosophes français comme Lavelle, Gabriel Marcel, Masson Oursel, Y. Wahl, Marcel Griaule ont porté des appréciations dans l'ensemble favorables au livre de Tempels" [Gaston Bachelard and French philosophers such as Lavelle, Gabriel Marcel, Masson Oursel, Y. Wahl, Marcel Griaule have in general provided a favorable appreciation to Tempels' book] (111). The book seems to owe its popularity to the fact that the ideas it provides are apparently opposed to the classical concepts and seem to inscribe themselves into one of the new parameters of the scientific spirit of the time: relativity.

Tempels understands philosophy as not being uniquely Western: philosophy has no absolute origin, content, or form. Other philosophies do exist and the Bantu people do have one. Tempels thus provides the means to show, by recurrence, that Negroes are not devoid of philosophy. Is Tempels' book blasphemous to the traditional Western philosophy that excludes Africa from the movement of philosophy—since Hegel and Levy-Bruhl relegate Negro consciousness to a pre-logical primitive mentality, incapable of philosophic reasoning? Tempels' theses seemed very advanced for the times.

However, a closer look reveals that the apparent rupture caused by *La philosophie* was actually continuity. Tempels does not understand philosophy in the same way Hegel does in terms of the world spirit progressing toward self-consciousness, the universal realizing itself in the Idea, or thought determining and giving itself a content. All that has nothing to do with the Bantu philosophy Tempels describes. His *La philosophie* is a perception of a world buried under proverbs, traditions, customs, and moral principles. He erects the Bantu's perception of the world into a philosophy that he translates. He appears as the interpreter, systematizing a collection of diffuse thoughts from a particular society into a philosophy for all Negroes.

Although Hegel's problem is not to know whether Negroes possess a world concept or a popular thought, Levy-Bruhl on the other hand counts on the idea of a system of collective representations proper to primitive communities. As for Tempels, he is not answering the question of an existing Negro philosophy following classical philosophic criteria. He simply puts off the problem. He makes a philosophy of the Bantu vision of the world, which he pretends to translate. Ontology thus is at the heart of the philosophy problematic.

Bantu or Negroes in general perceive reality through channels of thought different from European ones. While, according to Tempels, European thought is dichotomous and analytical, Bantu's thought consists of synthetic unity and transformation. In other words, they split over the antagonism between the static and the dynamic. Westerners see the world at rest, acknowledge and analyze it. Their philosophical discourse is based on the Being, which means all beings. As for Bantus, they conceive of the world in its mutations: its movement and all movements are a source of unfolding forces. *La philosophie* thus does not just *contain* ontology: it *is* ontology, a theory of forces. Tempels is very clear about the antagonism between the two ontologies:

> The Bantu thought in European language by saying that the Bantu speak, act, live as if, for them, beings were forces. Force is not for them an adventitious, accidental reality. Force is even more than a necessary attribute of beings: Force is the nature of being, force is being, being is force. We then think in terms of the concept "being," they use the concept "force." Where we see concrete beings, they see concrete forces. When we say that "beings" are differentiated by their essence or nature, Bantu say that "forces" differ in their essence or nature. (35)

Both Tempels' and Senghor's views appear as dichotomous and static as the Western one they describe. Their ontology is not just unitary, but existential. The force they talk about is life that has become force and animates beings and things. It is neither physical nor mechanical, but spiritual. For them, matter is not endowed with energy as understood by dynamic physics, but is an incarnation of living and transcendent spirits. Thus, Senghor writes: "Tout le système est fondé sur la notion de force vitale, qui, préexistante à l'être, fonde l'être. Dieu a donné la force vitale aux végétaux, aux minéraux, aux hommes: par quoi ils sont" [The whole system is based on the notion of a preexisting life-force which founds being. God has given vegetable, mineral, and human their vital force by which they are] (9). More categorically, he affirms that in Africa the apparent reality is the vital force. Therefore, the natural conclusion he draws is: "The African identifies *being* with life, or rather with the *life-force*. African metaphysics are an existential ontology" (36).

However, as Senghor says: "Le monde des forces est un système de vases communicants" [The world of forces is like a system of communicating vessels] (48), and that communicability supposes a system and an interrelation of forces that are not uniform but very hierarchical. That is why in the continuum of forces, Tempels' *La philosophie* places God at the top, and following, by order of importance, come the founding ancestors, the dead, the living, the animals, the vegetables, and minerals. For Senghor also, God is at the top and all forces converge toward him: "L'unité de l'univers se réalise en Dieu" [the unity of the universe is realized in God] (96). But if God is the high point of convergence of intricate forces, human beings occupy the center; so is Negro ontology anthropocentric. Tempels notes: "La création est centrée sur l'homme. La génération humaine vivante, terrestre est le centre de toute l'humanité y compris le monde des défunts" [All creation is centered in human beings. The living and terrestrial human generation is the center of the whole humanity, which includes the world of the dead] (45). However, it seems that the center that human beings occupy is subdivided into superior and inferior poles and White people all naturally are on the superior pole. Tempels writes:

> The White man, a new phenomenon in the Bantu world, could be conceived only according to pre-existing categories of Bantu thought. He was therefore incorporated into the universe of forces, in the position therein which was congruent with the logic of Bantu ontology. The White man seemed to be the master of great natural forces. It had, therefore, to be admitted that the White man was an elder, a superior human force, surpassing the vital force of all Africans. (44)

Unfortunately, Tempels did not live long enough to witness the historical contradiction of his theses in the form of bloody riots in the late 1950s: hundreds of White people were killed in the Bantu territories of Zaire and southern Africa.

Paradoxically, Césaire, one of Senghor's very close friends and intellectual partners, radically criticizes *La philosophie* as being as slimy and fetid as one can wish. He sarcastically writes: "This will have brought this miracle to pass: the Bantu god will take responsibility for the Belgian colonialist order, and any Bantu who dares raise his hand against it will be guilty of sacrilege" (59). For

Césaire, this is what it really says: "Let them plunder and torture in the Congo, let the Belgian colonizer seize all the natural resources, let him stamp out all freedom, let him crush all pride—let him go in peace, the Reverend Father Tempels consents to all that" (57-58).

Chapter Two

Contradictions in the Hegelian System

Such are Hegel's essential considerations: the geo-climatic environment explains Africa. For Hegel, the emergence of the spirit and therefore its development toward the Absolute is unfavorable to regions with extreme geo-climatic factors. He says: "The land surrounded by these mountains is an unknown Upland, through which [. . .] the Negroes have seldom made their way , except the Coast Tract, habitable only in a few isolated spots" (92). Next to it, we find "a girdle of marsh land with the most luxuriant vegetation, the especial home of ravenous beasts, snakes of all kind" (92) that no one can penetrate.

According to Hegel, such characteristics suffice to explain the African temperament and resistance to the emergence of the spirit. But let us not forget that according to Hegel also, natural, geographic, and climatic determinations are in no way fundamental. The spirit, in revealing itself through nature in order to give itself its own contradictory element and negative factor, shapes nature in its own form. In such a case, how can the spirit, even unconscious of itself, be at the origin of a nature that annihilates it?

It is conceivable that nature contradicts the spirit to the extent of making it fully reveal itself and thereby affirm its preeminence. But to present nature as totally capable of stopping the spirit's process of self-realization is to grant it a status that is not the one formally assigned to it. It also states that in the spirit there is a critical threshold of resistance against nature, which seriously questions its primacy in-itself. Or nature, like the spirit, has a status powerful enough to oppose the spirit and neatly triumphs over it, which Hegel will have difficulty to admit.

It could be that in the case of Africa the spirit is only a purely formal concept that Hegel uses to show that human beings are caricatures and not real persons. The latter proposition seems to be truer to Hegel's theses. The term "spirit" is then used only for Africa as an allegorical title. A dynamic reality, in-itself and for-itself, remains the exclusivity of known historical societies. It is not Hegel's explanations of climate and geography that are challenged; he is using them to mask—consciously or not—racist considerations on Africa. More than any determinant, he considers the Black race itself as a total explanation of the Negro character.

If so, we do not even have to insist on Hegel's errors and falsities in terms of the geography in Africa. It practically does not matter. Race is what is called into question and this happens at all levels, be it Africa, America, Asia, and even Europe. We then have to recognize that Hegel's subtlety consists in presenting his racism through profound but sure philosophical explanations whose sole purpose is to defend, illustrate, and legitimate Western imperialism in any way we look at it. In such a context, the Absolute spirit is only an hypostasis of the European spirit, determined by bourgeois aspirations to dominate the world and to absolutely seize the totality of Africa as shown by the slave trade and the dire exploitation of its raw materials. It is then no surprise that the French President Nicolas Sarkozy shocks African nations by reiterating this Hegelian notion of an unhistorical Africa during his 2007 visit in Dakar, Senegal. In his *Reuters* article, Diadie Ba quotes Sarkozy: "The tragedy of Africa is that the African has not fully entered into history. They have never really launched themselves into the future. The African peasant only knew the eternal renewal of time, marked by the endless repetition of the same gestures and the same words. In this realm of fancy [. . .], there is neither room for human endeavor nor the idea of progress."

For Achille Mbembé (2007) and most African thinkers, there are obvious similarities between Hegel's theses and the French President's speech. In an article published in *Le Monde diplomatique* (2007), the journalist Oliver Pironet echoes Africans' position: "the theses are steeped in Western arrogance and are a constant source of denigration, despite years of worldwide efforts to eradicate the prejudices that Africa has been confronting."

The Geographic and Climatic Determinism

It would seem that Hegel did not measure enough the extent of his theses on Africa, which leads him to internally contradict his own philosophy. Let us agree with him that the geo-climatic determinism is fundamental in Africa. To claim an unhistoricity of Africa in such a context is to affirm that geography and climate in Africa are essentially static. From such a point of view, the African geo-climatic space becomes an intangible reality, made up once and for all, indifferent to time, i.e. unhistorical. This position also assigns Africa a special status and totally differentiates it from the rest of the geophysical world, which according to Hegel is essentially dynamic in relation to the dynamism of the Absolute spirit in development. Does this mean that the spirit has not and *cannot* emerge in Africa because of its assigned configurations? We detect a double contradiction worthy of mention.

Earlier, we have underlined the first aspect: to present nature's possibility of freezing for ever the spirit in a state of itself is to deny the ontological primacy of the spirit, which is essentially dynamic. The following facts remain: if, as Hegel states, the spirit is the fundamental principle of the universe, if, moreover this spirit can only be conceived in the form of a dialectic deployment toward a self-realization in order to be absolute, if finally the universe exists inasmuch as it bears the mask of this spirit, it goes without saying that all social or natural reality can only be conceived in the form of this dynamism, proof of the absolute presence of the spirit in the world as a "system of reason." To consider only one part of the world immobile is not only to just limit the intrinsic power of the universal reason, but also its domain, thereby negating its absolute predominance over the sensual external world; this does not go well with the Hegelian system.

If the sensual external world constitutes an inferior order of the spirit as a reflection of its internal contradictions, it can be conceived in its totality only from a dynamic and developing angle. Indeed, at this phase, one can stress the fact that if the spirit is of a dynamic essence, it nevertheless retains its structure in-itself. It would then be conceivable that the sensual world contains in itself something invariable. It could be so, but there is a problem in terms of phases: at what stages of reality can one objectively determine a possible invariance in the external world? This is an important question. Providing a rigorous answer means to reveal the inherent contradiction in the Hegelian system concerning his theses on Africa and probably on other nations.

We must note that a perfect structure is kept within the spirit. The development is only a mode of actualizing that structure and does not at all imply an essential modification of the spirit's being. In precise terms, the forms of the spiritual structure change but not the spiritual content, which remains the same inasmuch as it defines the profound nature of the spirit.

However, this content is not abstract in its reality. In reality, one can only conserve it in the mode of a perpetual and progressive self-actualization. The principle of invariance is just that in its intrinsic nature the spirit remains spirit beyond the various phases of its development. The change is in fact only the process of the spirit's self-consciousness. What about the sensual world, which could be a substantial reflection of this spirit in development? It can only take the form of this spirit.

More precisely, it keeps the spirit in-itself as in the case of the atomic, cellular, or psychic structure, although these structures can only be retained by perpetually changing their formal content. Therefore, the atom goes from positive to negative and vice versa while still remaining a nucleus around which electrons gravitate, with at the base an energy going from concentration to deconcentration. Such processes simply mean that matter retains its structure no matter what the historical modalities of its existence are. This proposition can only be true in the determination of the external world *structure*. It remains inconsequent in terms of the determination of this external world's *forms*.

Geography and climate, more than anything, can only have formal contents, not structural, and are thus necessarily subjected to manifest or implicit changes. In their particular contents, geography and climate are external and superficial factors. They are ephemeral expressions of fundamental physical and chemical processes of the universe. Could a geographic or climatic reality last thousands of years, it still is no less important in the determinant process of change and evolution. Each continent has had various climatic and geographic eras, and Africa is no exception. The still ongoing desertification of the Sahara, once a fertile land, is a striking illustration of climate change. In this sense, it is illogical in Hegel's system to consider the Sahara static.

For Hegel, there is a certain determination to history and rationality to the world. Hence History is real because it is rational. It is rational because it is spiritual. If as such reality is the true expression of spiritual rationality, it goes without saying that the invariants of this spiritual rationality are only expressed in the fundamental, energetic, physical, and chemical structures of this reality. All other aspects remain secondary as the only concrete phases of the Absolute spirit's movement. It is then contradictory for Hegel to consider any variance in the frame of these phases in which the geography and climate are mostly obvious.

Moreover, to consider the geo-climatic sphere of Africa static and therefore socially unhistorical, inasmuch as this sphere is determinant, can simply denote in Hegel an empiricist outlook of things, which can hardly be concealed. He considers Africa as being and having always been as he describes it. Is not reducing reality to its immediacy the same as conferring it an impossible present with an immutable and eternal content? Yet, that is Hegel's process, which, besides his empiricism, remains totally speculative in regards to Africa, a place he never visited and whose true natural characteristics he ignores. In fact, this no longer denotes a secondary contradiction only but a structural one also. Hegel applies the same process to all other continents and nations. He considers them at a determinate moment of their histories and freezes them in geo-climatic considerations that are as fixed in terms of their contents. Indeed, Hegel insists on the determinant character of the climate, which is simply relative and secondary.

However, this is only stated from an intentional methodological point of view. Even if Hegel theoretically sees the spirit as determinant, he nonetheless considers the geo-climatic determinations essential; that is what makes him delimit the different activities of the spirit into as many natural zones. Consequently, only the temperate zones, and they alone, can be the theatre for the advent of the Absolute spirit. Therefore, hot and icy zones cannot in anyway serve as such. He considers such zones as having natural characteristics invariable in themselves as if it is in no way possible to detect important past or future variations.

Thus, when considering the various peoples of these zones, Hegel only classifies them by phases and at the same time locks them up in those phases. Strictly speaking, there is no history here. There is simply a graded classification of societies, which gives the impression of a history that is in fact only ideal. Ancient Greece succeeds Asia, which represents the dawn of the Absolute spirit; then comes Rome, followed by the Germanic nations as if these societies in their very essence forever represent the many moments of the spirit in development. However, these moments proceed from a sequence or a concrete process that is dialectic only in the unique sense of the spirit. It is as if nations are statically exposed here and there, and the spirit gets to each one in turn and inculcates a definitive essence in them.

Beyond the internal dynamic of pure Idea, we are reduced to an essentialist type at the level of sensual reality, which is an Aristotelian determination of peoples. There is a Europe and an Africa with no similarities at all, not because of a concretely different process of evolution, but because the spirit has definitely emerged in a different way on either side. This is a descriptive empiricism and "fixism" in terms of sensual reality and speculative idealism, considering the given explanation of this reality. These are the variants of Hegel's philosophy of history, which remains metaphysical and inconsistent in comparison to the real.

Such positions are and can only be those of an autarkic consciousness, impervious to the real that it glimpses through its architectonic but empty constructions. It is like trying to produce the concept instead of determining its foundation. Knowledge then is only a receptacle of speculations and conjectures in terms of sensual experience. It is precisely such a theoretical approach that forms the basis of any idealism, even a dialectic one such as Hegel's. The primacy of thought is stated a priori in the very process of reflection. The knowing subject undergoes a self-reversal independently of the already-considered secondary experience. Therefore, we arrive at either a negation of that experience or at erroneous considerations. The movement, thus, is no longer considered but a movement of thought, i.e. it remains a simple receptacle or a means of expressing thought.

However, we can ask ourselves to what extent this already idealistic dialectic is consequent with itself? The real as an expression of the rational implies that each element contains in itself a contradictory processes so that it aims at its proper internal surpassing. That is how fundamental contradictions are in things. Hegel himself emphasizes this in his criticism of traditional logic:

> But it is one of the fundamental prejudices of logic hitherto understood and of ordinary thinking that contradiction is not so characteristically essential and immanent a determination as identity; but in fact, if it were a question of grading the two determinations and they had to be kept separate, the contradictions would have to be taken as the more profound determination and more characteristic of essence. For as against contradiction, identity is merely the determination of the mere immediate. (439)

Hegel precisely falls into that "mere immediate" by considering Africa an immutable entity, always identical to itself, impervious to time and history. The dialectic contradiction implying movement and evolution remains impracticable in Africa. Here, it is the identity more than the contradiction that is fundamental in the hierarchy. There is just no particular reason for things to be so, if not that Hegel takes a great pleasure in gratuitous affirmations, which go against his very philosophical vision of world history. Moreover, contradiction implies that every aspect of reality must be considered as having its proper internal dynamic. Hegel himself says: "Contradiction is the root of all movement and vitality; it is only in so far as something has a contradiction within it that it moves, has an urge and activity" (439).

This internal dynamism defines the relationships that the most basic element maintains with other external elements. For this reason, external phenomena only have the status of secondary determinants and cannot at all be fundamental in the internal process of changing a given reality. Yet, such is not the position Hegel espouses vis-à-vis Africa. After denying the continent every internal possibility of movement and evolution, he naturally sets Africa's possibility to change in the unique context of exogenous interventions deemed determinant. The external determination becomes fundamental to the detriment of an internal determinant, practically inexistent in Africa, thus revealing once more Hegel's neat inconsistency with his dialectic. However, he remains consequent in his refusal to involve Africa in history. It goes without saying that if Africa does not have its proper internal dynamic, it can only be determined, in terms of a possible evolution, by other essentially historical and properly dialectic societies.

The fact that Hegel considers Africa as such remains unjustified and therefore arbitrary. If only his system included some principles of exception that allowed him such a theoretical attitude, there would be no objection; but that is not at all the case. Hegel remains fundamentally contradictory with his own system in terms of his theses on Africa. When they are not founded on geography and climate, they are essentially racist, and it would seem that, above all, Hegel's implicit racial considerations motivate his attitude.

Sociological Criticism

Within the context of human societies, it is inaccurate to consider geographic determinism fundamental. Hegel himself senses it but does not follow through. Thus, he formally replaces this type of explanation with the affirmation of an absolute determination of the Idea as the driving force of history. Geo-climatic determinism can certainly influence the social process but not unilaterally. Society in turn reacts in a certain way to climate and geography, which gives them a relative characteristic. In fact, there is a reciprocal influence between society and the environment. Human beings are not the finished products of their natural conditions of existence. These conditions do not determine them once for all, in the sense that human beings themselves have an effect on their environment when they master it to their benefit. This necessity to dominate or go beyond their natural conditions of existence is the proper characteristic of humans.

Within the African geo-climatic scope, this principle becomes more manifest, contrary to what Hegel thinks. The "torrid" characteristic of the African climate cannot prevent the human beings living in it from producing their own means of existence. On the contrary, this is verified in Sudanese Sahelian Africa, which interests Hegel so much in his denial of any history in the continent. Professor Pierre Fougeyrollas (1974) explains:

> Cette zone du continent africain est climatiquement caractérisée par des précipitations faibles aléatoirement réparties, bref, par l'aridité et la sécheresse. Comme l'ont noté les géographes, la saison sèche dure de 6 à 9 mois et les taux annuelles de pluie varient entre 500 et 1200 mm pour la zone proprement soudanienne, tandis que le sahel, rivage continental du Sahara, connaît des pluies inférieures à 500 mm et une saison sèche supérieure à 9 mois. Par là se trouve délimité en Afrique sub-sahararienne un gigantesque polygone de sécheresse où s'étagent, du Nord au Sud la steppe à épineux, la savane arbustive, la savane arborée et la savane herbeuse agrémentée le long des cours d'eau, par quelques forêts galleries et de loin en loin par quelques forêts parc. Il s'agit donc d'une vaste région de la planète où l'existence des collectivités humaines a dû et doit encore faire face à un permanent défi de la nature. [Random and weak precipitations, in short aridity, characterize this African continental zone. As geographers have noted, the dry season lasts from six to nine months and the annual rainfall varies between 500 and 1,200 millimeters, specifically in the Sudanese zones; while in the Sahel belt, rainfall is less than 500 millimeters and the dry season lasts up to nine months. Thus, a gigantic polygon of drought is delimited in sub-Saharan Africa, where from the north to the south, thorny steppes, areas of bush land, woodland, and the grassy savannah are like tiered. A few thick forest trees grow along the rivers and here and there, there are some forest parks. We are dealing with a vast region of the planet where the existence of human communities must have faced and is still facing perennial natural challenges]. (5)

It is precisely the human response to these natural challenges that determines the essential characteristic of African societies. It goes without saying that the first form of response is based on practices more or less close to nature. Thus, next to gathering, hunting, and fishing, which constitute the most human and archaic forms of struggle for life, we find mostly agriculture and animal breeding as privileged modes for traditional societies to dominate nature. These modes of coping vary from societies to society according to their geo-climatic situations.

The fact remains that in Africa, because of the drought, the response to the climatic challenge has been the most drastic and the reaction has taken several forms. Fougeyrollas states: "Lorsque le Sahara encore humide et fertile au temps du mésolithique et au début du néolithique est progressivement devenu aride et stérile, il en est résulté des migrations vers le Sud et vers le Nord qui ont donné au peuplement de l'Afrique son profil historique" [During the Mesolithic and at the beginning of the Neolithic periods, the still fertile and humid Sahara gradually becomes arid and sterile. As a result, migrations toward the south and the north have given the peopling of Africa its historic profile] (5). Even if these migrations are mechanical reactions, they nonetheless are a response to the arid natural environment and nomadic life, which characterizes most Northern African societies and giving it a real human form. This lifestyle, which consists in periodically moving about, is for these societies a means of keeping away from areas of extreme desertification and to reaching more bearable environments, such as oases.

Since these societies could not primitively fight the absolute aridity with any kind of agriculture, the idea has been to breed animals such as camels that can stand desert life, look for oases, and create humanly manageable conditions of existence. The less arid sub-zones offer the possibility of growing crops and breeding animals, among other activities. Thus, in Sudanese Sahelian Africa, agriculture has been the response to the geo-climatic challenge in the form of millet growing. Once again, Fougeyrollas explains:

> Le mil a été pour l'Afrique sub-Saharienne, l'instrument de la réponse au danger de la famine, comme le blé en Europe, le riz en Asie et le mais en Amerique ont été les moyens de vaincre dans la lutte pour la survie des peoples concernés. Le mil demandait un minimum de precipitations et il permettait un maximum de conservation. Grâce à lui, les communautés villageoises pouvaient demeurer sur leurs terroirs, éviter des migrations pénibles vers les zones premières et assimiler progressivement de nouveaux pasteurs nomades venus du nord-est [For sub-Saharan Africa, millet has been the answer to the threat of famine, in the same way that wheat has been in Europe, rice in Asia, and maize in America. Millet requires a minimum of rain and offers a maximum of conservation. Thanks to this cereal, village communities can stay on their soil and avoid painful migrations toward prime lands and gradually assimilate new nomad shepherds from the northeast]. (6)

The Race Problematic

Here again, it is first of all not only erroneous to posit a unilateral geographic determinism, but also inconsequent to consider race a dominant character. What interests us here are the implicit prejudices of Hegel's theses on Africa beyond what he says. We need to read between the lines and determine what Hegel is really implying.

The naturalness specific to the African spirit is intrinsic not because the Absolute spirit wants it to be so, but mostly because the African temperament absolutely allows it. Hegel's theses are obvious racial prejudices. The question is: can race be a fundamental determinant in the social process?

Racist scholars tend generally to argue that to each racially determined group correspond specific and structural characteristics, invariable through time and space, owing their consistency only to the group's biological structure, as with the Negroes. Thus, to the constitutive rationality of Whites would correspond rational social structures and a state organization. It would then be in the essence of the White race to be the conqueror and to impose itself by all means, dominate other nations, master nature, and thereby attribute reason to themselves as the most efficient instrument for such an undertaking. Naturally, science and technology are no longer anything but the inevitable results of White people's activities toward nature.

Therefore, White people set themselves up to be the superior biological type and sole true holders of civilization, which in the last instance is the only possible process for an efficient mastery of nature. White people, masters of civilization, are therefore the civilizing elements. The other races cannot do anything but be assimilated in order to gain their true humanity through the acquisition of the intrinsically White, scientific, and technical rationality. White people then acquire the necessary legal status, the indispensible and historic mission to humanize the other races and nations. If races have unequal capacities, then the superior one has to try to assimilate all other races, which legitimizes all the European undertakings vis-à-vis other nations.

On the theoretical level, such an argumentation, independently of its obvious ideological content, reveals a certain ignorance of the true nature of the social process. What in the first place determines the existence of a human society? The people. This is true for any society not adapting to nature but rather adapting nature to its needs. Such a process of adapting nature to one's self determines the emergence of a society. This universal phenomenon can be explained by the fact that the complex biological structure of humans determines their needs and interests, which cannot be satisfied by senseless nature, as they can with animals. This initial dissatisfaction is, *de facto*, like human immaturity with respect to their environment and needs. It is precisely to overcome such a situation, to mature, that humans set themselves about dominating nature and assimilating it to their needs. This process of maturation, by means of an effective mastery of nature, is at the origin of any human society, indeed of its structuration and ulterior evolution. Unlike animals, humans themselves create and produce their means of existence. Such a creation stems from the biological foundation we mentioned earlier, that is to say the qualitatively superior human constitution, which determines more complex needs, and wider capacities.

It is precisely at this level that racist points of view emerge. If it is the specific character of human constitution that is at the basis of social elaboration, it is understood that society is nothing more than a giant biological organization whose forms vary according to its groups' degrees of biological complexity. But this would ignore that the biologic specificity is only a necessary but insufficient condition in the elaboration of human society. The biologic formation is only indicative: it simply determines the possibilities of humanization and not a *de facto* humanity. Human biological structure changes when evolving in a purely natural environment.

The most striking example is Lucien Malson's and Jean Itard's *Wolf Children* (1976), and more interestingly, Jean Itard's *Wild Boy of Aveyron* (1962), whose protagonist became known as Victor of Aveyron. Victor spent his early childhood in the woods, among wolves; as a result, he used to emit raucous sounds like wolves instead of the sounds of an articulated language. His teeth were hypertrophied and he ate raw meat and walked on four legs, acting completely like a wolf though he was a human child. Indeed, as a little one, he only had a child's biological form. But that very form had been affected by the wild natural milieu in which he was living. He initially had in himself the preliminary conditions of a possible humanity. However, because of the lack of more fundamental ulterior conditions, he developed into a quasi-animal, and thus, into his own biological structure. Consequently, in the social process, the biological only holds a purely secondary status, an indicative determinant, necessary, but in no way sufficient. It is shaped by the social structures, which determine fundamentally it.

It is neither the biological structures nor race that determine social life. On the contrary, and along with Marx, I affirm that social life in its socio-economic structures is the determinant in the last instance, and not the biologic, whose real status is that it is an element of the social superstructure. Therefore, we acquire our thought, language and upright posture, and other organic characteristics from society. An individual is only socially human and not racially determined. He or she is, in Marxian terms, "an ensemble of social relationship" (150). It is not my quality of White, Black, or Red that gives me my human status. Rather, the level of social and economic structures proper to each society at a determined historical moment define the characteristics of the various human groups. The Negro's disposition in no way determines the characteristics of African society. That must be elsewhere, but not in the "African mind," which plays only the role of a simple superstructure. Otherwise, the struggle, which Africans have been through and are still going through, is universal. No one needs to demonstrate any longer the universality of physics, cytology, anatomy, organic chemistry, and their applications by medical technology. However, they do offer irrefutable proofs of the biological homogeneity of humankind, no matter what skin color or environment. To conclude with Marx:

> The life of species, both in man and animals, consists physically in the fact that man (like the animal) lives on inorganic nature; and the more universal man is compared with an animal, the more universal is the sphere of inorganic nature on which he lives. Just as plants, animals, stones, air, light, etc., constitute a part of human consciousness in the realm of theory, partly as object of natural science, partly as object of art—his spiritual inorganic nature, spiritual nourishment, which he must first prepare to make it palatable and digestible—so too in the realm of practice, they constitute a part of human life and human activity. Physically, man lives only on these products of nature, whether they appear in

the form of food, heating, clothes, a dwelling, or whatever it may be. The universality of man is in practice manifested precisely in the universality, which makes all nature his *inorganic* body—both in as much as nature is (1) his direct means of life, and (2) the material, the object, and the instrument of his life activity. Nature is man's *inorganic body*—nature that is insofar as it is not itself human body. Man *lives* on nature—means that nature is his *body*, with which he must remain in continuous intercourse if he is not to die. That man's physical and spiritual life is linked to nature means simply that nature is linked to itself, for man is part of nature. (67)

Despite our explanation of reason in history or *Philosophy of History*, our position, which continues to reveal itself in the next chapters, is that Hegel is not a racist. After more than eight years of research, Tavares is able to offer his findings to the world and in particular to African scholars. For him also, Hegel is not a racist and neither is anyone in his circle of friends. He refers scholars to the chapter on "Observation of the Relation of Self-Consciousness to Its Immediate Activity—Physiognomy and Phrenology" in the *Phenomenology* in which, using a mocking style, Hegel destroys the racist and racialist arguments of the time by tackling the pseudo-sciences of Physiognomy, Phrenology or Craniology. However, there is another aspect of his arduous work which delights us: he shows that Hegel has not authored any of the apocryphal and racially incriminating theses on Africa.

Hegel's enthusiasm for ethnic diversity may be seen as theoretically motivated in many ways. In this sense, Professor Joseph McCarney (2000) lends a hand by providing the following arguments on his behalf: "Racist assumptions are not merely otiose in Hegel's argument and lacking in textual warrant. They would also contradict the universalism of his philosophy of spirit with its central themes of freedom as the birth right of all human beings as bearers of spirit and of history as the process by which it is won for them" (145). Opposition and diversity are preconditions of a dialectical development and a historical process, which are themselves important aspects for a breaking free of the bonds of nature. Consequently, ethnic homogeneity appears as a direct expression of continued submersion in nature, of the still unchallenged grip of natural forces. McCarney draws our attention to Hegel's unequivocally firm position that world historical peoples are not to be thought of as ethnic groups thus: "He pours scorn on claims for the significance of racial purity, and insists instead on that of racial impurity, in spiritual development" (141).

Talking about "the beautiful free Greek spirit," Hegel says: "Of this principle, we must have a clear conception. It is a superficial and absurd idea that such a beautiful and truly free life can be produced by a process so incomplex as the development of a race keeping within the limits of blood relationship and friendship. The Greeks, like the Romans, developed themselves from a *colluvies*—a conflux of the most various nations" (226). As for the Germanic world, it has remained backward until they started to open up to the outside. Hegel says: "Only then did their development begin, kindled by a foreign culture, a foreign religion, polity, and legislation. The process of culture they underwent consisted in taking up foreign elements and reductively amalgamating them with their own national life. Thus their history presents an introversion—the attraction of alien forms of life and the bringing these to bear upon their own" (341-42).

Like Tavares and Dieng, McCarney has not come across any suggestion—biological or theoretical—that Africans are of inferior stock. He says: "There is, however, no room in Hegel's vision for radical and elemental divisions between human groups as racists characteristically propose. Indeed, a firmer theoretical basis for the fundamental equality of human beings that Hegelian spirit provides can scarcely be conceived" (145).

We believe that Hegel—swimming in superior thoughts—is not a racist and cannot be so. He understands his world—our world—too well to be bothered by petty thoughts. According to Tavares, Hegel has never made any secret of his anti-slavery stand and thus has always been a friend of humanity. He is an eagle and not a cackling chicken, as Wilhelm Reich would say. We agree that he knew Africa as much as the information of his time allowed him. He describes Ancient Egypt as the land of marvels but located it in Asia, the Oriental world. For Dieng, the findings of scholars such as A. R. Bidja, Tavares, Augustin Dibi Kouadio, and Peter von Armin are making it difficult to maintain that Hegel is a racist.

Hegel may still be caught faulted for his premises since he locates Egypt—land of the pharaohs—in the Oriental world. Nevertheless, Egypt is where one finds a spirit that feels pushed to exteriorize itself, but only in a sensitive manner. Hegel describes the Sphinx:

> Of the representations, which Egyptian Antiquity presents us with, one figure must be especially noticed, viz. *the Sphinx*—in itself a riddle—an ambiguous form, half brute, half human. The Sphinx may be regarded as a symbol of the Egyptian Spirit. The human head looking out from the brute body exhibits Spirit as it begins to emerge from the merely Natural—to tear itself loose therefrom and already to look more freely around it; without, however, entirely freeing itself from the fetters Nature had imposed. (199)

Chapter Three

The State and Civil Society

For both Marx and Hegel, the state appears to be the summary, the condensation, in short, the quintessence of political reality. Hegel's and Marx's theories of the state are the response that they bring to the general problem of human alienation. We bring out the significance of the state in general according to them and place it against the state in Africa in particular.

State and Freedom: The Hegelian Concept of the State

Hegel's understanding of the state is very complex. We limit ourselves to a brief examination of the significance of the state according to him in order to shed more light on the African scene. His definition of the state is very original. For him, external criteria—the geographical environment, relationships, and common economic interests, among other things—do not command or define human beings that belong to a state. The state is the only formation whose existence is connected to the human will, which belongs to it. The state is the organization in which we must live. It is not a "materialist" society in which a blind necessity compels individuals to organize themselves at random and for fear of extinction. Hegel, thus, dismisses all the "naturalist" concepts of the state. For theorists of "natural laws" such as Thomas Hobbes (1651), the emergence of the state formation is linked to a so-called state of nature in which human beings struggle to immediately and completely satisfy their selfish individual interests. They lead a true *bellum omnia contra omnes*. In *Leviathan*, Hobbes says: "Hereby it is manifest that during the time men live without a common power to keep them all in awe, they are in the condition which is called *war*; and such a war as is of every man against every man" (95). From such a perspective, the state emerges at a time when individuals become aware of the eventuality of a total loss of the human species and decide to get along and stop destroying each other. Thus, the state is only a result or a crystallization of a pact that has been made between individuals. Hegel radically criticizes such a concept that eventually leads to founding the state on irrationality.

However, Hegel's criticism does not discard Hobbes' basic scenario. For Shlomo Avinieri (1972), if for Hegel, "The state becomes necessary at the moment when society seems to be heading for disruption and chaos," then "the basic scenario of Hobbes is, in a way, being re-enacted here" (99) in a different context. Indeed for Hegel, the citizens' will constitutes the state authority. However, their will must be understood in another way than that of a subjective one.

Jean-Jacques Rousseau also devotes himself to finding the foundation of the state. He deals with the question in terms of the general problem of relationships between the private individual will and the general one. And Hegel's very problem lies in the perspective of such a general problematic. Rousseau's answer is familiar. It is a variation of the "naturalist" solution in the sense that for Rousseau, also, the state is the fruit of a "social contract" by which individuals freely decide to limit their particular interests to subordinate them to the general interest:

> The first and most important consequence of the principles established above is that the general will alone can direct the forces of the state according to the object of its founding, which is the common good; for if the opposition of private interests has rendered necessary the establishment of societies, it is the concord of these same interests that has rendered it possible. That which is common to these different interests forms the social bond; and unless there were some points in which all interests agree, no society could exist. Now, it is solely with regard to this common interest that the society should be governed. (170)

In his criticism of the Rousseauist concept, Hegel does recognize Rousseau's merit of having rid political thought of empiricism, i.e., the idea of a "social instinct" or a "divine authority" as the foundation of the state. He says: "The merit of Rousseau's contribution to the search for this concept is that, by adducing the will as the principle of the state, he is adducing a principle, which has thought both for its form and its content, a principle indeed, which is thinking itself, not a principle, like gregarious instinct, for instance, or divine authority, which has thought as its form only" (156-57).

However, Rousseau's concept is still insufficient in the sense that it does not clearly, meaning rationally elaborate on the notion of will. The idea of the "social contract" does not explain the essence of the state. It is just a stratagem that does not really allow the reunification of the private and general wills. The notion of the contract still retains in itself the arbitrary: it is valuable only to those who explicitly recognize its authority on them. Therefore, it is not universally normative or "objective."

Rousseau maintains the principle of the individual will in the sense that the existence of the state depends on its members. That is where Hegel sees the expression of a lack in grasping the very essence of the state. The incomprehension comes from the fact that consists of starting from nothing or from an abstract ideal state, and which exists only in the individual's imagination. On the other hand, Hegel wants to start from the notion of "political virtue, the willing of the Absolute existing in itself and for itself" (155). In other words, he starts from the fundamental idea that the necessary existence of the state—not any particular state, but one from a universally recognized order—is inside the universal reason itself. Talking about Rousseau's concept of the state, Hegel states:

> He takes the will only in a determinate form as individual will (as Fichte did later), and he regards the universal will not as the absolutely rational element in the will, but only as a general will, which proceeds out of this individual will as out of a conscious will. The result is that he reduces the union of individuals in the state to a contract and therefore to something based on their arbitrary wills, their opinion, and their capriciously given express consent. (157)

He further says: "Confronted with the claim made for the individual will, we must remember the fundamental conception that the objective will is rationality implicit or in conception, whether it be recognized or not by individuals, whether the whims be deliberately for it or not" (157).

Hegel much less accepts the extreme concept, according to which the state is only a creation of a purely historical coincidence, which is Carl Ludwig von Haller's position, which Hegel bitterly criticizes. According to Paul Franco (1999), Haller's *Restoration of Political Science* (1816 and 1820) provides the theoretical justification for a critique of social-contract theory and a defense of natural-divine order based on inequality and the relationship of domination and dependence. While Rousseau "takes natural domination as the basis of political authority instead of 'thought' or human freedom," Haller sees "Political authority as emphatically 'not human' but, rather, 'rooted in nature' as an expression of the will of God" (288). By excluding the notion of what the state should be from his theory, the Restoration philosopher, or Herr von Haller, as Hegel calls him, also prevents any possibility of criticizing historic states. One refrains from saying what states should not be. For Hegel, any theory that aims at "restoring" any state is an avoidance of thought and its consequent rational use. It is not a coincidence if in his tentative restoration Haller does not bring in notions of laws and rights at all, because they are the essence of the state, its ideal and conceptual content. Moreover, to diminish or purely and simply ignore the importance of such notions equals mutilating the profound meaning of the state.

Such a blunder, according to Hegel, is not an innocent one. It follows a political prejudice, which leads to a step backward, to the state as it is conceived in the Middle Ages. Indeed, one cannot fight for justice in the state without first setting up notions of laws and rights, which constitute its substance. The opposite boils down to a capitulation in the face of blind violence and political oppression justified and sanctified by God's will. Such a doctrine naturally leads to a subordination of politics to religion, and the state to ecclesiastic authority. Therefore, justice becomes a fortuitous act of grace that Princes have in their possession from some kind of divine delegation. Subjects then become the King's absolute private property. Hegel thus harshly criticizes Herr von Haller's position, which legitimizes the domination of human beings by political powers and moreover attributes the reign of injustice in the state to a religious spirit. Hegel says:

> Her von Haller might have discovered by his 'religious feeling' that he should rather bewail his condition as the hardest chastisement of God. For the hardest thing that man can experience is to be so far excluded from thought and reason, from respect for the laws, and from knowing how infinitely important and divine it is, that the duty of the state and the duties of the citizens should be defined by law—to be so far excluded from all this that absurdity can foist itself upon him as the word of God. (160)

Thus, Hegel definitely answers a question that he raises himself in his early writing: the relationship between religion and politics. Not only does he admit the separation between the two, but he also thinks that the conditions of freedom reside in the subordination of religion to politics. Such a criticism of the dominant political concepts of his time gives us a sufficient idea about the significance of the state in relation to human freedom.

It is necessary to remember that for Hegel the state is an Absolute necessity. For him, it is impossible to live outside of a state. Everybody, in the end, must find a comfortable and freely acceptable state formation to which one can willingly submit. That is why he sees in the different states that succeed each other in history milestones or the necessary moments in the process of realizing a total human freedom.

Thus, the dialectic of the state identifies itself with the dialectic of freedom and not with an arbitrary one as in society. The dominant notion of freedom in Hegel's early writings is here fully explained: it is the free will seeking its own freedom. However, in Hegel's perspective, the state essentially has a moral signification. He says: "The state is the actuality of the ethical idea. It is ethical mind *qua* the substantial will manifest and revealed to itself, knowing and thinking itself, accomplishing what it knows and in so far as it knows it" (155).

The state is not located at the level of the simple possibility of freedom: it wants real freedom. The state not only requires that its members attain a status consistent with human dignity, but also and more profoundly that the balance between rights and duties must be guaranteed. Moreover, the state is not identical to particular organizations that stem from traditions such as the family or social and professional groups. The state does not act according to subjective rules of freedom, but it knows that it must realize freedom, and all its actions are subordinated to this goal. The state then reveals itself as morale of the people made manifest in the sense that it expresses the will of the people out of which it has emerged.

To a certain extent, one can say that for Hegel the state assumes a divine character which does not at all imply the idea of transcendence. He says: "For the state is not an abstraction, which stands in opposition to the citizens; on the contrary, they are distinct moments like those of organic life, in which no member is either a mean or an end. The divine principle in the state is the Idea made manifest on earth" (95).

The state is thus a "substance" maintained by its proper strength; but this strength consists in the individual's recognition of the supremacy of the public interest. Hegel distinguishes between "piety," which is a subjective virtue and "political virtue," which defines the relations between the citizen and the public life within the state. In so far as the state is an organization, which its members want, and since this will demands that they renounce the arbitrary in favor of universal freedom, the state represents the highest level of realizable rationality in terms of social and political life.

More precisely, the state, which coincides with reason, is capable of realizing its will. No human beings can elevate themselves to such a level of freedom. Only within the state can freedom be a valid norm for everybody and be respected as such. This freedom, by definition, excludes all partiality. It is a universally valid norm. For precisely this reason, belonging to a state is more than a necessity; it is an absolute duty, which must be entirely guided by reason. Moreover, it does not, in any way, identify itself with an external order or injunction that reduces itself to a blind obedience. Hegel says: "This substantial unity is an absolute unmoved end in itself, in which freedom comes into its supreme right against the individual, whose supreme duty is to be a member of the state" (156).

However, the individual interest *per se* is not the goal of the state, which should not be subjected to a material calculation: the state complements individuals and allows them to reach a full moral fulfillment. In other words, the individual or subjective morale is at the same time an individual's promotion. Thus, individual morale is founded on a practical and subjective need. As such, it cannot process any universalizable normative value in the sense that it comes up against other subjective needs, which are each claiming supremacy. The normative and universalizable character of all these subjective needs and desires can only stem from the concrete universal that is the state. However, the state as a crystallization and materialization of the subjective morality—if it is indeed the product of the consent of the individuals living within—also appears in the form of an obligation that weighs on them. The state holds the necessary moral strength to force itself upon those who consent to it.

As we can see, for Hegel the fundamental goal of the state is to put an end to individuals' isolation and to confer a meaning on their lives by integrating them into a social totality. That is the only way for an individual who is part of the communal life to find a true satisfaction. Here we discover the young Hegel's central theme of Greece as the ideal from which he defined freedom as an adequacy or harmony between the subjective element (the individual) and the objective element (the city). Hegel puts it this way: "The subjective will—or passion—is the activating and realizing principle; the Idea is the inner essence, and the state is the reality of ethical life in the present. For the state is the unity of the universal, essential will and the will of the subject, and this is what constitutes essential life" (94). Thus, the essence of the state is an ethical life, which consists in the unity of the universal and the subjective will.

We can ask ourselves whether individual and universal wills do unite in the state. For Hegel this unity realizes itself in the state because the identity of the goals to attain is realized in the state itself, in the actions and means by which these goals make themselves manifest. More precisely, the law presents itself as the universal mean of realizing the goal, and that is why, by substituting itself to the private rule, it eliminates any possibility of disagreement between the universal and the particular wills. Hegel says:

> Rationality taken generally and in the abstract consists in the thoroughgoing unity of the universal and the single. Rationality, concrete in the state, consists (a) so far as its content is concerned, in the unity of objective freedom (i.e. freedom of the universal or substantial will) and subjective freedom (i.e. freedom of everyone in his knowing and volition of particular ends); and consequently, (b) so far as its form is concerned, in self-determining action on laws and principles, which are thoughts and so universal. (156)

Therefore, the law, by its universal character, allows the realization of the unity of free private wills and institutions, which aim at satisfying and guaranteeing the particular interest of these multiple wills. Reasonable action is well thought out by its very nature, i.e., it is the result of a lucid thought. Therefore, it is not impulse that guides it but fundamentally the concern of realizing something permanent, something that exceeds individual limitations. That is why universal activity (the state's) cannot be subordinated to a private rule but must only be carried out by a means equally universal: the law. More precisely, for Hegel, the realization of freedom in the state is essentially a matter of *prise de conscience*. Thus, in the establishment and functioning of the state, the consciousness of freedom is determinant. It gives an irrecusable meaning to its institutions and is therefore the supreme force.

For Hegel thus, individual freedom is only possible in and by the state, but never outside. The state is the very rationality that has become reality. Its essence envelops its existence, so to speak. In Paul Franco's (1999) words: "For Hegel, the nation-state was central to the achievement of freedom in his understanding of it because it is within the nation-state that we find the normative structure that can give meaning and salience to freedom. We do not find freedom in a wholly private and voluntary existence withdrawn from the public world of politics and nationhood. It is found through belonging to a nation" (389).

By considering the state to be the manifestation of the Idea on earth, Hegel places it above any suspicion of injustice or irrationality. By making the realization of freedom the state's fundamental goal, Hegel is naturally led to justify and legitimize the means of activity by which this goal can and must be achieved: the law.

The objectification-alienation of particular wills in general (subsumed by the state) is far from meaning human beings' dispossession. On the contrary, it constitutes their elevation by allowing them to rise from singularity to universality. Or even better, by and in this elevation, the singularity is not suppressed but is preserved within the universal, which has become concrete.

Hegel thus develops a real apologetic concept of the state. It seems that his notion of basing the state on ideas of liberty and equality of citizens is inspired by the ideals of the French Revolution. However, it is remarkable that in his theory Hegel no longer includes the third ideal of "*Fraternité*." It is because for him the idea of fraternity is not a proper category that falls under the concept of freedom. In the same way he considers piety—which dominates the world religious vision—a subjective virtue, purely personal or "pathological" in Kantian language.

Does this mean that the state realizes perfectly its ideals? In reality, the state necessarily contains differences and even inequalities, in the sense that various parties form it. However, one cannot reject these inequalities without at the same time rejecting the whole state. For Hegel, the realization of an absolute inequality is *a priori* excluded. It is a mistake to found human freedom and equality on "natural right." In reality, human beings are rather unequal "by nature."

Thus, the egalitarian principle does not depend on human "nature": it is the most abstract expression of rational law. Hegel says: "This single abstract feature of personality constitutes the actual *equality* of human beings. But that this freedom should exist, that it should be *man* (and not as in Greece, Rome, etc. *some* men) that is recognized and legally regarded as a person, is so little by *nature*, that it is rather only a result and product of the consciousness of the deepest principle of mind and of the universality and expansion of its consciousness" (266). He goes on: "Therefore, laws—expression of the abstract rational right—are necessary to resolve problem and conflicts that stem from the natural inequality of human beings" (266).

For Hegel, the ambiguity in the notion of freedom comes from the fact that it is made up of two aspects: the objective and the subjective. The objective aspect of freedom is the law, which grants a right against the duty it requires. It is this aspect that Hegel retains to justify his idea of the state's goal of guaranteeing freedom to all citizens. He says: "Really, every genuine law is a liberty: it contains a reasonable principle of objective mind; in other words, it embodies a liberty." (266)

However, one can ask whether the state, by imposing laws on the citizens, does not maintain them in some form of servitude. Do not the relationships between governors and governed become reduced to one of command and obey? Are not ideas of freedom and equality simple illusions that certain categories of individuals invent to mask and render domination acceptable? For Hegel, to ask such questions is to be mistaken about the true meaning of the state laws: "On the contrary, it should be said that it is just the great development and maturity of form in the modern state that produces the supreme concrete inequality of individual in actuality" (267).

However, Hegel thinks that modern states, which maintain within themselves certain forms of inequality between individuals, can at least give themselves the means to correct or considerably diminish or even totally suppress this state of facts. He says: "Through the deeper reasonableness of laws and the greater stability of the legal state, it gives rise to greater and more stable liberty, which it can without incompatibility allow" (267).

This precisely means that the role of the state consists in giving free rein to the citizens' personal evolution, their particular interests, and then integrating them into the whole with laws that lay down each one's rights and obligations. By allowing diverse personal liberties, the state wants and can satisfy everybody's freedom. There is thus a whole dialectic of recognition between individuals and the state, which first implies that they do not feel state interests as being fundamentally opposed to theirs.

Moreover, individual initiatives must not be smothered and their participation in public affairs must be encouraged. However, this formulation—that the state does not stand opposite private initiatives—only gives the negative aspect of the individual's recognition of the state. The positive aspect consists in recognizing that the state is really the domain of individual satisfactions and that consequently it is worth contributing to the state's wealth and greatness. Therefore, individuals must have the feeling that the state needs them, that their contributions are essential, and that they must not retire from public life as persons whose ultimate goal is to defend their own private interests against the state's. Hegel recognizes the following: "The principle of modern states has prodigious strength and depth because it allows the principle of subjectivity to progress to its culmination in the extreme of self-subsistent personal particularity, and yet at the same time brings it back to the substantive unity and so maintains this unity in the principle of subjectivity itself" (161). Hegel constantly resists the idea that the essence of the modern state is to "reconcile" subjective freedom with the conditions that the existence of the total state requires.

We have seen in Hegel's early analysis of the political and religious ideal how he sought to justify the city-states of antiquity. In his later work however—particularly in the *Philosophy of Right*—he is going to recognize the progress that the modern state has achieved in relation to the ancient state in the sense that in the latter, the defense of the collectivity takes precedence over the personal liberties'. He says: "The essence of the modern state is that the universal be bound up with the complete freedom of its particular members and with private well-being, that thus the interests of family and civil society must concentrate themselves in the state, although the universal end cannot be advanced without the personal knowledge and will of its particular members, whose own rights must be maintained" (280).

Identity in difference are the key words in Hegel's concept of the state. However, the state that Hegel advocates is nothing other than the liberal republican type of the modern bourgeois state. More fundamentally, we can say that the Hegelian concept of the state constitutes a speculative transposition of the alienation issues. Indeed, his concept is much more of a political philosophy than a true political theory. What he proposes—to think the state out—is less to analyze or describe the state in its concrete determinations than to think out its essence. The state is only a mediation by which the Idea makes itself manifest on earth.

In the last analysis, what can we retain from the Hegelian concept of the state? Absolute knowledge is the advent of individual freedom exerting itself in a state that has itself overcome all scissions. Thus, we arrive at the realization of the divine on earth. At this particular time, the Prussian state represents the most perfect expression of Absolute spirit. The most valuable and virtuous aspects have triumphed. In the end, the spirit has realized itself because Hegel thinks that eventually the history of the world is the Last Judgment of the world.

Hegel also considers the state the very actualization of freedom. The state institution, which is the concrete and historical reality, derives its existence from the Idea itself. As we see, Hegel rejects Rousseau's concept of the state: the state is the common will, the expression of conscious and individual wills. Such a state is in fact historic therefore capable of being altered, transformed, and of dying.

Thus, the Hegelian state is of a divine character. It is absolute authority, absolute majesty. The state is for Hegel the general and rational will in itself and for itself. He says: "The patriotic sentiment acquires its specifically determined contents from the various members of the organism of the state. This organism is the development of the Idea to its differences and their objective actuality" (164). The spirit or the Idea is eternal and since the state is the perfect embodiment of the Idea, it is eternal.

Such a conception is speculative but does reach its goals: the disruption of the Prussian state is no longer conceivable for the human spirit. Therefore, one of Hegel's major preoccupations is resolved. There no longer is a need to nostalgically evoke the beautiful and harmonious Greek city because: "The principle of modern states has prodigious strength and depth because it allows the principle of subjectivity to progress to its culmination in the extreme of self-subsistent personal particularity, and yet at the same time brings it back to the substantive unity and so maintains this unity in the principle of subjectivity itself" (161).

Historical Reasons and the Renunciation of the Revolutionary Ideal

Thus, Hegel's fundamental problem—which leads him to break away and distinguish himself from transcendental idealism—is the elimination of any duality between the ideal and the real, between freedom and necessity as the unavoidable outcome of the development of the historical reality of his time. Indeed, his time is the point of articulation between the agonizing feudal era and the era of Enlightenment which announces a whole new society with the French Revolution. Hegel recalls these precise moments:

> The spirit of the time, growing slowly and quietly ripe for the new form it is to assume, disintegrates one fragment after another of the structure of its previous world. That it is tottering to its fall is indicated only by symptoms here and there. Frivolity and again ennui, which are spreading in the established order of things, the undefined foreboding of something unknown—all these betoken that there is something else approaching. This gradual crumbling to pieces, which did not alter the general look and aspect of the whole, is interrupted by the sunrise, which, in a flash and at a single stroke, brings to view the form and structure of the new world. (75)

Or in the *Philosophy of History*:

> The conception, the idea of Right asserted its authority *all at once*, and the old framework of injustice could offer no resistance to its onslaught. A constitution, therefore, was established in harmony with the conception of Right, and on this foundation all future legislation was to be based. Never since the sun has stood in the firmament and the planets revolved around it had it been perceived that man's existence centers in his head, i.e. in Thought, inspired by which he builds up the world of reality. But not until now had man advanced to the recognition of the principle that Thought ought to govern spiritual reality. This was accordingly a glorious mental dawn. All thinking beings shared in the jubilation of this epoch. Emotions of a lofty character stirred men's minds at that time; a spiritual enthusiasm thrilled through the world, as if the reconciliation between the Divine and the Secular was now first accomplished. (466)

However, the very process of historic development—with the French Revolution and industrialization—reveals new, unexpected, and disturbing elements that would contradict Hegel's previous understanding. They completely modify the vision Hegel has so far had on the development of things and life. Indeed, from 1793, at the time Hegel has leaves Berne for Frankfurt, he witnesses the Jacobin dictatorship and its fall on 9 Thermidor (July 27, 1794). Hegel notices with dismay that the French Revolution has ceased to represent general interests and has become the expression of the interests of a well determined and particular class: the bourgeoisie that is now trying to seize political power to solidly assert its class domination. In Germany, the problem of unity that Hegel has so much desired arises with more acuteness since the French Revolution reaches Germany in the form of a military occupation.

All these events become a true historical drama. Despite the surprising contradictions in the technological progress itself—mechanization and alienated labor—they traumatize Hegel, shattering his spirit. These are heartrending, unexpected, and mortifying events. Eventually, deception and discouragement lead Hegel to lose the revolutionary enthusiasm that he felt during the preceding period. A true change occurs in his thought and he starts to express a resignation to the impossibility of a German unity. Roger Garaudy (1962) quotes Hegel: "Les pages suivantes sont la voix d'une âme qui, à contrecoeur, dit adieu à son espoir de voir surgir l'Etat allemand de son insignifiance et qui, avant d'abandonner complètement ses espoirs, une seule fois encore voudrait se rappeler vivement ses désires de plus en plus faibles et jouir une seule fois encore de sa faible foi en leur accomplissement" [The following pages are the voice of a soul that reluctantly says goodbye to its hope of witnessing the German State spring out of its insignificance. But before completely abandoning all hopes, it would like to one more time vividly remember its fading desires and one more time indulge in its weakening faith in their realization] (10).

Hegel also detaches himself from his first position, his first vision of reality, and the world. Indeed, with the fall of the Jacobin dictatorship, Hegel realizes the illusory and Utopian nature of his Hellenic dream: social reality can no longer be considered a living totality carried by individuals as foundations of their lives and singularities. Moreover, terror becomes the expression of powerful antagonisms between the different parts of the totality that is social life.

We witness the development of civil society, a sphere which now separates the individual from the state and in which only private interests prevail. This civil society is the world of corruption, maneuvering, cunning, savage covetousnesse, and constant unfulfilled desires. The split between individuals and state reveals itself in the total loss of the meaning of the state. Only particular wills matter. Thus, Hegel is led to see a victory over terror and liberalism in the dictatorship of Napoleon, whom he calls "the world soul on horseback."

However, the anarchic situation in civil society develops in Hegel feelings of "the absolute necessity of a governmental power. Napoleon restored it as a military power, and followed up this step by establishing himself as an individual will at the head of the State: he knew how to rule, and soon settled the internal affairs of France" (470). Therefore, Hegel relinquishes his conception of the modern state being the event of reason, the unity of concrete freedom and individual subjectivity. It is the supersession of the antic state, which is the immediate unity of individuals and society. It is also the event of Christianity in which individuals are withdrawn into themselves and are separated from a society that has now become an external reality to them.

As for Germany, Hegel realizes that the internationalization of the French Revolution, which he had thought to be the triumph of Reason and an all new world, born from the ruins of a feudal and oppressive world, has become a series of wars of aggression, conquests, and plundering. Instead of bringing happy modifications into the social and political system—particularly the unity of the German nation—these wars reinforce the feudal forces themselves, particularly in Austria and Prussia. This part in Hegel's life is well summarized by Robert C. Solomon (1985):

> His [Hegel's] unabashed liberalism took a shock as the revolution turned to terror. Napoleon crowned himself emperor, became the invader, an autocrat, desperate, and finished at Waterloo. While Hegel ruled the philosophical roost in Berlin, the government came down hard on students and the very sign of "freethinking" in the universities. This was the period of Metternich, the crushing of liberalism, rigid control of the press and education in general, broken promises for reform, secret societies, omnipresent police surveillance, culminating in a series of revolutions across Europe in 1830-31 put down by Metternich, whose influence was slowly corroded by the beginning of the industrial revolution and rise of the German bourgeoisie and working class. The economic liberalism that Hegel had studied with enthusiasm as a young man, began to catch hold in Germany. (17)

Marx's Historical Foundations of the State

In terms of economic life, Hegel notices that the introduction of the machine has undoubtedly provided humans with inestimable advantages in the sense that labor is less hard and painful and an important work can be done in a considerably shorter time frame. He also recognizes that civil society, the battlefield of private interests and furious competition, is rationally founded. But for Marx, the total freedom that constitutes Hegel's goal of the state is not from a concrete domain but rather from a speculative abstraction. To what extent is the Hegelian concept of the state a "true" solution? The Marxian concept of the state provides answers.

The Marxian concept of the state is essentially a criticism of Hegel's philosophy of politics, rights, and the state. As we have seen, in his analysis of the state Hegel starts from an ensemble of philosophical presuppositions, with the main one being that the state is the necessary and crucial moment in the realization of reason as freedom. He ends up making civil society a simple phenomenal manifestation of the Idea and the state, their concrete realization. Marx sees in such a conclusion an "idealist" inversion, which consists in explaining a concrete reality with the Idea. Thus, Marx sets out to invert the Hegelian inversion and to "put it on its feet" by explaining the notion of the state in terms of bourgeois society, which he considers to be the only concrete reality. This inversion contains all the criticisms Marx levels against Hegel's idealism, which presents the state system in an inverted form.

For Marx, the true, concrete, subject bearer of predicates is the social human being which belongs to civil society. The predicate of this concrete human being is in fact the state, which Hegel wrongly considers the subject, or the Idea made manifest. The Idea, which is in fact produced by the social human being, appears in Hegel's as the authentic subject. From here, according to Marx in *La sainte Famille* (1969): "C'est une mystique qui dégénère en mystification" [it is mystique that degenerates into mystification] (163). Therefore, in the Hegelian philosophy of the state, there is a juxtaposition of pure logic and empiricism that Marx denounces. He underlines the transitions through which Hegel goes: from a development of the pure Idea, valid in his logic, to a concrete reality that could be both the organism, in term of biological life, and the constitution, in terms of political life. The question then is: if Marx denounces the philosophical presuppositions that dominate Hegel's concept of the state, is he not replacing them with another presupposition of his own?

Contrary to Hegel, Marx wants to locate analytical thought in the real historical ground. Instead of thinking out the concept of the state, the question is to positively analyze the essence of the state by connecting it to its objective foundation, which is the economic stage. Such is Marx's fundamental presupposition from which he wants to start his analysis of the political reality and the state in particular. From such a perspective, Marx thinks of studying the problem of the state in its historical relations with the economic conditions of existence and forms of appropriation.

To the state forms correspond private properties throughout history. The state has not always existed but has appeared because of certain determined historical circumstances. Marx says: "The modern French, English, and American writers all express the opinion that the state exists only for the sake of private property" (77). Therefore, the state is only the expression and reflection of the social economy at the political level.

Thus, Marx radically lodges a challenge against all theories—particularly Hegel's—that place the state above the social economy and the interests it develops. Marx ruthlessly criticizes the Hegelian concept in which the state is the means by and in which private interests (individuals' or groups' interests) and the general interest are reconciled. For Marx, this conception, which leads to a justification or worse, a sanctification of the state, masks an illusion that turns into a mystification. For Marx, not only is the state not above particular interests that appear in civil society, but also its whole reality is founded and explained by such interests.

The state is never an innocent and rational element, which fully guarantees the total freedom and equality of all its citizens. The existence and reality of the state is founded on the existence and reality of social classes whose interest are fundamentally antagonistic. The state stems from the impossibility of a true conciliation, much less a re-conciliation, of these interests. More precisely, the state is an instrument that a determined social class gives itself in order to protect its interests and exert dominance over other social classes. Therefore, the state corresponds to an objective necessity of organizing the economically dominant class. Marx says: "By the mere fact that it is a class and no longer an estate, the bourgeoisie is forced to organize itself no longer locally, but nationally, and to give a general form to its mean average interest" (77).

Contrary to Hegel's view, the state is not the concrete universal that is above class oppositions, which the pursuit of selfish particular interests creates in civil society. The state stems from this civil society that in turn explains it. Marx says: "The term 'civil society' emerged in the eighteenth century, when property relationships had already extricated themselves from the ancient and medieval communal society; civil society as such only develops with the bourgeoisie; the social organization evolving directly out of production and commerce, which in all ages forms the basis of the state and of the rest of the idealistic superstructure" (76).

However, for Marx each new class ascending to power is compelled to give its common interests a universal form. The state thus appears to Marx as an enormous mystifying construct. He says: "Since the state is the form in which the individuals of a ruling class assert their common interests, and in which the whole civil society of an epoch is epitomized, it follows that the state mediates in the formations of all common institutions and that the institutions receive a political form. Hence the illusion that law is based on the will and indeed on the will divorced from its real basis—on free will" (78).

However, it seems that the state has acquired a particular existence next to and outside the civil society. The concrete form of the state administration stands opposite the individuals that have become abstract. That is why the state, far from realizing human beings' freedom, consecrates their alienation by turning them into mere abstract citizens, subjected to the domination of the law. The alienation is more frightening as the abstract (the state) tends to detach itself from the concrete basis (civil society), and to turn against it. Therefore, the state becomes free in relation to society and leads a quasi-independent existence, while struggling on two fronts: against the proletariat, its internal enemy, and against other nations or states.

Nevertheless, politics, the state, rights, or institutions do not each have their proper history. They develop by and thanks to the economic movement and that is the fact that they become autonomous—by alienating themselves—that gives them a semblance of particular and independent existence. All four structures are built on the basis of the structure of civil society and become estranged from the economic life, and alienate the people living in it.

The scaffolding that they erect maintains people and things "in their place," preventing them from developing all their potentialities. All the political, state, administrative, institutional, and juridical development takes place above individuals' heads, so to speak. In the extreme, people only appear as simple supports of the state structure. Here, we find again what Hegel has already criticized in the name of positivity:

> When civil society is in a state of unimpeded activity, it is engaged in expanding internally in population and industry. The amassing of wealth is intensified by generalizing (a) the linkage of men by their need, and (b) the methods of preparing and distributing the means to satisfy these needs, because it is from this double process of generalization that the largest profits are derived. This is one side of the positive. The other side is the subdivision and restriction of particular jobs. This results in the dependence and distress of the class tied to work of that sort, and these again entail inability to feel and enjoy the broadened freedoms and especially the intellectual benefits of civil society. (150)

The state, as product of human thought and activity, becomes an estranged power, which exacts its domination over the very activity and thought that have given it birth. That is why Marx strongly unmasks the abstraction (bearer of illusions) of laws and rights: juridical laws only express economic laws in a distorted form; it is a mystification. Right are the rights of the dominant class, which it guarantees. Organic life, which is the effective society of those who work and live in community, falls under the domination of the state and its stifling rights. Leaving the social ground, the state develops its own logic, betrays universal interest and only looks after the property owners' interests.

In light of the above explanation, we can better understand Marx's radical criticism of Hegel's political thought. Yet, we must say that Marx's criticism of Hegel starts from Hegel's own knowledge of political philosophy, whose truth Marx recognizes insofar as he grasps well the essence of society and the history of modern society: private property. However, Marx accuses Hegel of understanding the ideal essence, genesis, and development of the state apparatus and laws, their function and power, but not their effective truth, their true genesis and history, which therefore are material.

The state and law remain spiritual beings since the spirit is the only true being of the state. Thus for Hegel human beings' political alienation within civil society and its state—separate realities—is maintained and justified. Real and alienating political existence thus remains concealed. It only reveals and suppresses itself in thought and philosophy. However, political philosophy can in no way overcompensate for the reality of the political drama. Insofar as political alienation is the alienated expression of economic alienation, Marx thinks that Hegel's political philosophy—as an ideological expression—is itself a third-degree alienation. That why he writes: "Hence my true religious existence is my existence in the *philosophy of religion*; my true political existence is my existence in the *philosophy of law*; my true natural existence, existence in the *philosophy of nature*; my true artistic existence, existence in *the philosophy of art*; my true *human* existence, my *existence in philosophy*" (141).

Therefore, the existence of political alienation is practically maintained and surpassed in theory. Marx says: "The man who has recognized that he is leading an alienated life in law, politics etc., is leading his true human life in this alienated life as such. Self-affirmation, self-confirmation in *contradiction* with itself—in contradiction with both the knowledge and the essential being of the object—is thus true *knowledge* and life" (140).

Although Marx knows how to grasp the scope, magnitude, and depth of Hegel's political philosophy—without 'buying into' the disparaging and superficial judgments formulated against him—he still does not cease to ruthlessly criticize Hegel. Hegel has expressed in a philosophical language the non-true truth of civil society, the state, and politics of his time by raising the real existence to the level of truth, transforming the rational into the real and the real into the rational, and seeing the latter incarnate itself into the former. Hegel thus avoids the development of modern society, i.e., the one leading to the necessity of a revolution, which will definitely suppress the state and the political alienation it carries.

Thus, contrary to Hegel, Marx does not want to stop before the supreme reality of contradictions, but he denounces them. He does not just want to surpass them for a superior abstract unity; he wants to suppress them. Marx shatters the existing contradictions between the state's fictitious totality and human beings' organic totality, between citizens and human beings, and political life and generic life. In the name of historical "realism" and materialism, he denounces everything that dominates the effective society

For Marx, bourgeois relations have given birth to a "juridical and political superstructure," a state. For Hegel, economic liberalism, civil groups, and bureaucracy are only a moment of the true Idea: the State. The modern state for Hegel resolves the problem of the unity of individual liberty and general will. However, for Marx the state does not phenomenalize the Idea. On the contrary, it is the instrument that the dominant class—the capitalist bourgeoisie—uses to perpetuate its domination over the proletariat. Marx thus gives the state a purely economic meaning. He writes: "Religion, family, state, law, morality, science, art, etc., are only particular modes of production, and only fall under its general law" (91).

Marx criticizes Hegel for juxtaposing pure logic to concrete and historical reality. Indeed Hegel passes the development of the pure Idea to concrete and historical reality. Therefore, Hegel's thought is formal and speculative: he substitutes the logic of the thing with the thing of the logic. He says: "The State is the Divine Idea, as it exists on earth. We have in it, therefore, the object of history in a more definite shape than before: that in which freedom obtains objectivity" (41).

This Hegelian mystique seems to be a mystification in itself because by trying to insert the concrete and contradictory reality into the logic of the Idea, Hegel seems to try to justify the unjustifiable. The State is not the materialized rational and the rational is not real. The idea that Hegel is affirming, according to Marx, "est précisément en contradiction avec la réalité irrationnelle qui est partout le contraire de ce qu'elle exprime et exprime le contraire de ce qu'elle est" [precisely contradicts the irrational reality, which is everywhere the opposite of what it expresses and expresses the opposite of what it is] (134).

The religious sphere is comparable to the political one. They are both illusory realities. The political sphere transcends individual realities and forms itself into an abstract and autonomous entity. Hence a dualism, a split between the state and civil society, and bourgeois and citizens (the *Declaration of the Rights of Man and of the Citizen* (1791) perfectly illustrates this split. Human beings are not the citizens and the citizens are not human beings.

If the modern state is the perfect embodiment of human beings' generic being, individuals or private human beings are abstracted and alienated because they are thus deprived of their generic being: the state is the imaginary and illusory materialization of the generic being of humans. No matter what monarchic or feudal form it takes, the state is always the same. That is why Marx says: "The struggle between monarchy and republic is itself a struggle within the *abstract* state. The *political* republic is democracy within the abstract state form. The abstract state form of democracy is therefore the republic; but here it ceases to be the *merely political* constitution" (21).

According to Marx, in civil society real life appears dead; the split between the general and individual interests is indeed to the profit of the particular interests of the bureaucratic society. Individuals thus renounce their social and communal being to only focus on their private, arbitrary, and selfish interests. Marx says:

> The perfected political state is, by its nature, the *species-life* of man as *opposed* to his material life. All the presuppositions of this egoistic life continue to exist in *civil society outside* the political sphere, as qualities of civil society. Where the political state has attained to its full development, man leads, not only in thought, in consciousness, but in *reality,* in *life,* a double existence—celestial and terrestrial. He lives in the *political community,* where he regards himself as a *communal being,* and in *civil society* where he acts simply as a *private individual,* treats other men as means, degrades himself to the role of a mere means, and becomes the plaything of alien powers. The political state, in relation to civil society, is just as spiritual as is heaven in relation to earth. It stands in the same opposition to civil society, and overcomes it in the same manner as religion overcomes the narrowness of the profane world; i.e. it has always to acknowledge it again, re-establish it, and allow itself to be dominated by it. Man, in his *most intimate* reality, in civil society, is a profane being. Here, where he appears both to himself and to others as a real individual he is an *illusory* phenomenon. In the state, on the contrary, where he is regarded as a species-being, man is the imaginary member of an imaginary sovereignty, divested of his real, individual life, and infused with an unreal universality. (34-35)

Political emancipation, as we have seen, is far from being perfect. Human emancipation cannot be realized through an intermediary. Human beings cannot emancipate in and by the state, for intermediary means separation. The state separates humans from their freedom. Marx says: "Thus, political emancipation is not the final and absolute form of human emancipation" (32). Just as with religion, the state expresses human limitations. The state in fact expresses humanity's practical struggles in the same way religion expresses theoretical struggles; political power is the official summary of civil society's antagonisms.

Nevertheless, is not trying to suppress all contradictions and realize total unity—for such is the goal of the criticism of the state—a proof of idealism? For Marx effective and total freedom is linked to the suppression of the state. Can this goal be just a romantic notion of unity or a dream of totality made manifest? Is not such a global vision of the world tinted with idealism? One wonders whether Hegel does not give the impression of being more realistic than Marx, since he does recognize and accept the necessity of mediations and alienation. It must be what Professor Duncan Forbes (1975) is referring to when he says: "In criticizing Hegel, [Marx] thinks he is doing this, but his critique is such that even when he has apparently played havoc with Hegel's alleged contradictions, the deeper rational meaning of the modern state suggested by Hegel's dialectic still stands. The fact is that Hegel's front-line is more advanced than it need be, beyond the sheer logic of freedom" (xxxi).

To better understand Hegel's and Marx's concepts of the state, one has to see how they relate not only to human beings' social and economic life but also to the problem of alienation, which we are not per se addressing here.

We have shown that for Hegel and Marx, the history of politics is tightly connected to economic developments. Hegel conceives his state as a solution to the problem of human freedom, on the basis of the necessity of surpassing civil society. After him, Marx has conceived the necessity of such a development, but only by extending it to the state itself. The movement of the Marxian dialectic is nevertheless as realistic as Hegel's, particularly as an analytical critique. Just as Hegel does, and maybe more than him, Marx constantly explains political reality by going back to its fundamental root and taking into account the emerging contradictions, which unfold in the economic sphere.

State and Social Structures in Africa

The problematic of social structures and class struggles in Africa directly refer to the emergence of the state in Africa. However, because Hegel has denied historical development to Africa, this study will use Marx's understanding of the state—with all the Hegelian components—to explain its emergence in Africa. Moreover, the chaotic situation of modern states in Africa compels us to ask what is the root cause of all these conflicts and who benefits from them. With such considerations in mind, Marx's contribution to the understanding of the state reveals itself suitable to explain the emergence of the state in the particular case of Africa. The Marxian state also happens to be African countries' understanding of statehood. Because of their nature as former European colonies, the notion of the state is perceived as an ongoing antagonism between rich nations and poor nations, or between the national bourgeoisie and the proletariat, made up of workers and peasants.

Therefore, we begin by accepting the fundamental fact that the state is never more than the political instrument of an economic domination. Its particular form in Africa is not "the Idea of the Spirit in the external manifestation of human will and its Freedom" as Hegel suggests. On the contrary, Marx sees that the existence of the state—no matter at what level—necessarily indicates differentiated or protagonist social classes. For Marx, "the state exists only for the sake of private property" (187). His perspective is to study the state issue in its historical relations with the economic mode of production and forms of property. Since the state is the form in which the concerned groups assert their common interests, "it follows that the State mediates in the formation of all common institutions and that the institutions receive a political form" (187).

Therefore, the state is only the expression and reflection of the socioeconomic reality at the political level; hence its role as the political instrument of an economic domination. Its structures and functions are comprehensible only when related to the social and economic situation, which it aims at consolidating. The state is only the organic expression of the contradictory process of production and reproduction of the means of existence, characterizing all class societies. Therefore, the state is explicable only in reference to a society's internal movement. Frederick Engels explains:

> The State is, therefore, by no means a power forced on society from without; just as little is it "the reality of the ethical idea," "the image and reality of reason," as Hegel maintains. Rather it is a product of society at a certain stage of development; it is the admission that a society has become entangled in an insoluble contradiction with itself, that it is cleft into irreconcilable antagonism which it is powerless to dispel. But in order that these antagonist classes with conflicting economic interests might not consume themselves and society in sterile struggle, a power seemingly standing above society became necessary for the purpose of moderating the conflict, of keeping it within the bounds of 'order,' and this power, arisen out of society, placing itself above it, and increasingly alienating itself from it, is the State. (158-59)

However, as far as Africa is concerned—although the definition applies—the determination of the state emergence also seems more complex. For authors such as Samir Amin (1978) or Catherine Coquery-Vidrovitch (1991), external or international commerce have given birth to the emergence of African states and more precisely to African empires, particularly in the Sudan. Their position seems to be supported by the fact that, on the one hand, these states have maintained solid trade relationships mostly with Arabs and partly with Europeans; on the other hand, Marx theoretically supports their position in his *German Ideology*, stressing the "civilizing effect of trade expansion and the intercourse of nations" (182) in accelerating capitalist accumulation. Consequently, Maurice Godelier (1975) affirms: "In West Africa, the emergence of the Ghana, Mali and

Songhai empires . . . seems to be linked to the tribal aristocrats' control on the exchange of precious products, gold, ivory, skins, etc. between Black and White Africa" (30). Amin and Coquery-Vidrovitch eventually systematize this position. By just sticking to the structural content of such affirmations, we find a neat consequence in relation to Marxist theory's fundamental principles. Marx says: "it is simply wrong to place exchange at the center of communal societies as the original, constituent element" (239).

The refutation of this exogenous position is now the goal of a second group of scholars, advocates of endogenous causes, such as Dieng (1975), Pathé Diagne (1976), and ethnophilosophers: they see the positing of commerce, circulation, exchange, and merchant relationships as incapable of founding any social structure whatsoever. Unless one perceives it from an empiricist position, these elements are certainly dynamic, and therefore influential, but they are only simple secondary effects. Nevertheless, they are external forms of more fundamental structures. These scholars' argument—citing Marx—is that production is the basis of all social and economic formation. It is the basic economic nucleus, which—in its internal dynamic—shapes circulation, exchanges, and consumption, which are only derivatives. Therefore, they think that it is theoretically erroneous to believe exogenous forms of activity can generate an internal social process. They argue that asserting external phenomena to be determinant with respect to any social or natural reality would be ignoring dialectics and materialism. In their view, each society necessarily has its own auto-dynamic internal structures. Therefore, to explain such dynamism by external phenomena reveals a deliberate ignorance of the notion of internal dynamism *per se*. In so doing, the exogenous position rejects Africa's real history.

Moreover, when the exogenous position stipulates that the law of supply and demand is a fundamental dynamic in Africa, it is accused of falling in the trap of justifying the capitalist exploitation of developing countries. It makes the mistake of explaining flagrant relations of exploitation between capitalist powers and developing countries as just a "deterioration of the terms of exchange"(7), as Amin says. Such social and economic theory of international relationships is mercantilist and assumes that rich and poor countries are equal partners and that only the terms need reworking. To affirm, as Amin does, that external commerce gave birth to African states is to deny any proper historical initiative to Africa.

According to the endogenous position, such a perspective, considered from the political angle, is the justification needed by foreign powers to intervene in Africa, supposedly either to "free African people" or "get them out of under development." For Dieng, the exogenous position is just another form of African-Hegelianism: "Many scholars professing the most contradictory ideas agree to give international commerce an important role in the formation of the great Sudanese empires. This thesis, at the end, denies all historical initiatives of great importance to black people and is hinged with a racism that does not always appear frankly" (30).

Both trends may be Marxist, but they seem to forget the flexibility and inclusive aspect of dialectics. If one is solely looking at Africa, endogenous elements are the source of the state in Africa. Thus, such a position makes it sound like the continent is some kind of self-sufficient island with no connection to the rest of the world. If Africa is an integral part of the world, then its truth does not reside in itself, in its own history, but in the historical system which contains it. Therefore, if the advocates of exogenous factors see one historic process and not several, it is because as Marx explains in the *Grundisse* (1973): "While capital . . . must strive to tear down every barrier . . . to exchange and conquer the whole earth for its markets, it strives on the other side to annihilate this space with time" (538-39), or, "Capitalism—its movement in time and space—is the process, which *universalizes* the particularity of its multiple contents and establishes a worldwide, *unified historic processs*" or: "Manufacture and the movement of production in general received an enormous impetus through the extension of commerce, which came with the discovery of America and the sea-route to the East Indies [the trade with African kingdoms and the trans-Saharan routes]; and above all, the extension of markets into world the market, which had now become possible . . . called forth a new phase of historical development" (182).

I can understand ethnophilosophical scholars trying to credit a historically discredited Africa, but the reality of the continent is both internal and external, and more external than internal. Marx continues to explain: "There are highly developed but historically less mature forms of societies in which the highest economic forms are to be found, such as cooperation, advanced division of labor, etc., and yet there is no money in existence" (388). In *Marxist Theory*, we touched on Economy not existing in pre-colonial Africa, using Engels's definition of Economy: "Political economy came into being as a natural result of the expansion of trade, and with its appearance elementary, unscientific huckstering was replaced by a developed system of licensed fraud, an entire science of enrichment" (151).

Our point thus is that Economy could not be in the reality of African pre-colonial/medieval societies simply because it is a theory of merchandise from the point of view of the state; it is the preliminary or at least the concomitant existence of merchandise as a dominant social relationship that necessitates Economy. We know that money and merchandise as social rapports only held a marginal place in pre-colonial Africa. Marx explains: "Money as well as exchange to which it owes its existence, does not appear at all or very little within the separate communities, but it appears on their boundaries in their intercommunal traffic" (388). Nevertheless, money begins to play its part everywhere at an early age. Even if it did not pervade all economic relations in Africa, African aristocracies must have become daily less and less able to do without it. They eventually become more involved in it and their activities become absorbed into the world market.

If African kingdoms had been bustling markets, as we explained in the introduction, then there must have been reciprocal actions between production and commerce. It is understandable that such tremendous international activities may have triggered the formation of the state, which allowed the city-states to maintain their status as regional and international centers. Arab, but mostly European invaders just made sure that African states were modeled on theirs. In so doing, they globalized Africa.

African states are thus part of the worldwide commerce and repartition of production. They are dependent on an international market, which is concentrated in a monetary system. These kingdoms—now independent States—must only try to place their local economies in the world market. They represent very logically the world market at the local level. Thus, Africa is dominated by international capital and its endogenous elements cannot change this situation.

Chapter Four

Fundamental Aspects of African Cultures

African thought is generally defined by a certain number of principles. In this work of categorization research, scholars have thus far derived bodies of concept from references and comparisons to "Western reason." Such an approach is illegitimate if intellectuals think that they can reach from it a specificity in-itself of African thought, in relation to all the possible forms of mental operations. However, it can be justified if it is considered only a first moment of a general process and does not lose sight of other poles of comparison, which could bring some points of specificity into the universal sphere. By appropriating the principle of comparison as a first step here, we aim at continuing in the footsteps of our predecessors—while refining and drawing out what specifies Negro African thought in the usual comparison to Western thought.

What Negro African Thought Is Not

The fact that African thought is not generally in written form is not enough to conclude that it is something diffuse, non-systematic, or unconscious of itself as often described. One can adopt such a thought only if one swims in a Hegelian a priori. In such a view, African thought—asleep, alienated and, buried in priests' and wise men's discourses—only reaches self-consciousness later on and through the philosophical age process. Hegel says: "What we properly understand by Africa, is the unhistorical, undeveloped spirit, still involved in the conditions of mere nature, and which has to be presented here only as on the threshold of the world's history" (99). So it is with the Hegelian Absolute spirit, which can transcend the state of self-unconsciousness only in its stride through temporality, the beginning of a dialectic movement, the continuous renewal of the spirit-matter opposition, or the dramatic crossing of multiple stages. Hegel says:

> The development of the consciousness of Freedom on the part of Spirit . . . implies a gradation—a series of increasingly adequate expressions or manifestations of Freedom, which result from its idea. By [the] very process of transcending its earlier stages, gains an affirmative, . . . a richer and more concrete shape—this necessity of its nature, and the necessary series of pure abstract forms which the idea successively assumes—is exhibited in the department of *Logic*. (63)

In this general problematic, one cannot espouse the idea of an unconscious thought, buried under myths, metaphors, or formulas because the simple or complex social praxis that it reflects, is itself conceived as such. Therefore, there is neither an African thought unconscious of itself because not expressed by philosophers who are conscious of the nature of their discourse, nor an unconscious Negro African praxis, incomplete in itself.

What about the notion of a unity or "symbiosis with nature" dear to Senghor? From Jacques Maquet's (1967) principle of Negro harmony with reality, we learn:

> Africans obtained the material goods they needed not so much by conquering nature as by submitting to it. Untamed nature, the forest, the savannah, the bush, surrounded the hunting band's camp; the farmer's field the lonely village. Nature, which man can never ignore, is vast and indifferent, it hurts as much as it protects, and the good man as often as the bad man is in turn victim and beneficiary. Unlike Westerners, who, having succeeded in defying, proceed toward its complete subjugation, African seeks harmony; they achieve it by sharing in its life and strength. This is the material basis of what has been called the Bantu philosophy of vital force (63-64).

Thus, according to Maquet, nature hurts or protects humans and the individual has no choice other than to be one with the whims of such a nature. This position is untenable and if so, brings the reflection down to the simple level of praxis. One is unable to explain certain violence perpetrated against nature by Negro Africans: the digging of a hole to find a water source, the violence against the mineral or vegetable during fieldworks, or the destruction of game for consumption. These few examples seem to represent so many Promethean deeds for or against the taming of nature and so many violent forms of materializing ideas or thoughts. In short, they refute the supposed harmony Negro Africans would have with the cosmos.

There is another side of the notion of unity, which stems from the variation when one establishes correspondences, analogies, or homologies between totalities or the different levels of reality. We know that such an operation is far from being limited to Negro African thought: in Western thought, is not Surrealism—in its Baudelairian version—one of its manifestations? The principle of dividing would be the opposite of the principle of uniting. Based on the idea of isomorphism, which appears frequently between the organization of thought and languages, experience tends to reveal that there cannot be a social human language that does not categorize reality to affirm itself as such. Viktoria Yartseva (1977) explains: "in the Russian lexicon, the word 'depeo' also designates an arborescent plant as well as the material, which is 'bois' in French, 'wood' in English, and 'holz' in German" (95). The Tamacheck of northern Niger classify the colors bleu and green under the same term 'tazzawzawt' to be opposed to the other natural colors such as 'tarwq' [yellow], 'takwalt' (black), 'tamlat' [white], and 'tazwaq' [red] (96). Therefore, each thought makes a categorization, indeed specific but just the same, a categorization of reality.

Negro African thought would also be mythic, mystic, and symbolic and would exclude the alternative. According to the philosopher Alassane Ndaw (1975), it would be so in the sense that it refers to myths to explain a reality in which it operates by "pratique divinatoire pour expliquer les phénomènes nouveaux non intégrables dans des types" [divinatory practices to explain phenomena, which cannot be integrated into types] (18). For Ndaw (1978), in Negro African thought, "l'exclusion de l'alternative aurait pour conséquence la force du caractère sacré des principes et exclusion de toute possibilité d'une remise en question" [the exclusion of the alternative would lead to a strengthening of the sacred character of principles and to elimination of all possibility of questioning] (105). The symbolic character would then form the basis of the "subsistence de la croyance malgré le démenti de l'expérience" [the subsistence of the belief despite the reality contrast] (105), which would characterize Negro African thought.

Mircea Eliade (1975) and Bronislaw Malinowski (1985) among others abundantly explain the origin and function of myths. Suffice it to say that myth is an appendix of experience. The mythic and mystic interpretation of reality has always supplemented objective knowledge as the expression of its limitations, an escape and anticipation of reason. It is also a reaction, from that same reason, to the limitations that experience imposes. Understood as such, mythic, mystic, and irrational interpretations cease to be the preserve of Negro African thought.

Does the exclusion of the alternative remain characteristic? The category of the alternative is an integral part of the concepts of true and false, which underlies any possibility of choice. Now, in Negro African traditions, these two concepts do exist and can be reversible in the language. What has been considered true can cease to be so under the weight of objections to become the non-truth or 'fen' [lie] in Wolof. Thus Negro African thought does know the category of the alternative. The movement or the dialectic historicity of myths and their reciprocal exclusion in African mythology, supports this thesis.

The degree of remoteness in the praxis also offers another criterion for specification. In this regard, we think that African myths, tales, proverbs or popular maxims seem to be much closer to human needs and social relationships than the operations of a Western state religion or other ideologies, which reduce direct experience to a representation.

Of Negro African Art

African art covers vast areas such as literature (poetry, fiction, theatre), cinema, music, song and dance, painting, engraving, sculpture, gold and silversmith, and architecture among others. Robert Thompson (1997) adds: "Tropical Africa has elaborated a different art history, a history of dance art, art danced by multimetric sound and multipart motion" (17). Susan Vogel's *African Aesthetics* (1986) explains that in Africa, artists seldom portray particular people, actual animals, or the actual form of invisible spirits. Rather, they aim to portray ideas about reality, spiritual or human, and express these ideas through human or animal images. Thompson adds that with African art "We enter, in other words, a code, a stylized form of consciousness, involving all in deep and primary vitality" (17).

A possible typology can reveal two domains. The first, African traditional art, was born out of hundreds of distinct cultures that have created over a thousand different art forms in a style that expresses long established customs. This original art is not found in urban areas but in the hinterland. The second and other art was born from the meeting of African civilizations with others, in particular the Western world. As a hybrid form, this art distinguishes itself from Western canons with difficulty, in form as well as in content. Therefore, the question is: is there a unity, a specific and common background or a profound relationship among the diverse Negro African art forms?

One main argument is that the goal of African art is to consider beauty from the perspective of the societies that produce these arts. In his *Conscience et communication esthétique négro-africaine* [*Consciousness and Negro African Aesthetic Communication*] (1975), Ndaw thinks that European tradition tends to use Greek aesthetics as model. However, he sees another kind of beauty that is not solely or simply based on harmony and measurement. He says: "Si l'on veut comprendre vraiment le problème de la creation et de l'esthétique africaines, il faut les situer dans le milieu où elles se posent effectivement et non dans une perspective occidentale [If one really wants to understand the problem of creation and African aesthetics, one must be placed in the environment in which they actually arise and not in a Western perspective]" (5). Vogel among others supports Ndaw's position. She asks: "What are the criteria for evaluating African art? Who establishes them? What are they based on? Are they the same as those of the artists who created the work, or of their patrons? Clearly the criteria we use are our own, formed by late twentieth-century sensibility and informed by the study of African art" (xi).

On March 1977, at a conference on *Teaching Philosophy*, the Société Africaine de Philosophie (SAP) [African Philosophical Society] refutes the affirmative answer. The SAP's point is that in Negro Africa, one can distinguish three large groups, each one with its proper characteristic style: the Sudanese (West Africa), the Benin-Yoruba-Sierra Leone to Cameroon, and the Equatorial or

Bantu (East Africa) groups. However, under these unities, one can easily detect an infinite variety: a Baoule mask or a Bambara statuette. The SAP also recognizes a repertoire of functions that are usually considered specific to African art: magic and religious, therapeutic, pedagogical, and social entertainment and esthetic functions among many others. According to the SAP, in the hierarchy of functions—and in connection with Western creation—African art would rely less on the category of form. Thus, the problem in African art is more of content (signification, functions, and uses) than form. For the SAP, the European observer is usually struck immediately, by the geometrical structure of objects, the abusive simplification. We must stress here that instead of merely copying nature and the real, the artist gives more importance to some elements or certain aspects of the real, which are thus emphasized, exaggerated.

The observation that we can make here is that Western art ignores none of the functions enumerated above. Wole Soyinka's intervention at the *Abidjan Colloquium on Negro African Theatre* (1970) supports this argument by showing the structural similarity between Greek and Negro African tragedies. In terms of good and evil, existence and transcendence, human responses—be they Greek or Yoruba—are the same: Thou shall not kill or steal etc. For him, Shongo (Sky Father, God of thunder), Ogun (God of thunder, fire, iron, hunting, war, and politics), and Zeus have the same status: they watch over the world order.

Although Vogel advises consideration of beauty from the perspective of the societies that have produced these arts, she nevertheless, recognizes that African art reflects a moral universe in which the beautiful and the good are combined— aesthetic form and aesthetic content. She puts it, "Given this moral foundation, it principal subject is the human figure, as it was for the Greek, whose art also has a moral base" (xiv).

For Allan Shields (1973), it is a confusion to believe in the total distinguishability of Black intellectual successes from some other kinds of intellectual human successes. For Shields, there are "no Black aesthetics because "one cannot meaningfully speak of 'Black' trigonometry, 'Black' organic chemistry, 'Black' physical exercise, 'Black' nature studies, or 'Black' logic" (319). His argument is that, "though there is a limited sense in which Black aesthetics can be meaningfully used as a concept, this sense is trivial and inconsequential and there is no serious, supportable meaning of a *theory* of Black aesthetics as distinguished from general aesthetic theory" (319).

This position seems difficult to adopt for many African scholars. The *Abidjan Colloquium*, the *Yaoundé Colloquium on Criticism*, and the second *Abidjan Colloquium on Negro African Literature and Aesthetics* (1976), believe in the existence of a Negro sensitivity: a human way proper for African to perceive the beautiful. Their point is that opponents of Negro aesthetics are victims of the imperialist Western intellectual tradition: Plato, Aristotle, Kant, and Hegel have provided a dogmatic and metaphysical definition of aesthetics. Their second argument stresses the growing interest in traveling to Africa—Baudelaire, Nerval, and Rimbaud—and the influence of African art via Europe in the 1920s:

artists such as Vlamick, Matisse, Modigliani, and Picasso have been profoundly influenced by basic concepts in traditional African art.

African scholars in general think that one can always find a general trend in Negro African creation, a common thread, which reveal its profound particularity—besides the categories linking it to universal norms and thus subject to the exigencies of academic definitions. Are not Negro Africans' particular styles of singing, shouting, and speaking giving a strong testimony to the belief in a distinctive Negro feeling? Hasn't Black music (blues or Jazz) influenced this or that aspect of Western art in general? It is an African people's art for Africans while being the product of its creator.

In recent decades, the efforts of all colloquia so far have been to systematize the notion of a Negro African aesthetic with the understanding that African art, no matter what the form or aim, is communal. It is an integrated tool in the process of production, instead of being, at times, an object of contemplation. Ajumé H. Wingo (2004) clearly explains this social dimension of African art: "In this conception of art, what makes a piece of work an artwork is not merely who made it, where it was made, and what it was made of, but, more importantly, whether it can invite people together. That is, more is required in Africa to give something the status of an artwork—a room full of people, for example, invited by an artwork" (426).

However, Negro-African art is not specified by the list of functions that the SAP enumerates or by a so-called ignorance of the category of form, and much less by a finality of being "an expression of life." In this matter, Ndaw offers a dialectic approach: "There is no difference between *content* and *form*. From a Negro art perspective, there is never an empty form" (115). In other words, the form is the content, which has become concrete. Without form, the content of the work ceases to exist. As for art as an "expression of social life," I maintain that that is integral to all art. Art always reflects society. Therefore, like any other art, Western art forms inform us about life as much as they reveal themselves after being psychoanalyzed—if they do not so empirically—as a total social phenomenon. Otherwise, it is just as Hegel says in his *Aesthetics*:

> The universal need for expression in art lies, therefore in man's rational impulse to exalt the inner and outer world into a spiritual consciousness for himself, as an object in which he recognizes his own self. He satisfies the need of this spiritual freedom when he makes all that exists explicit for himself within, and in a corresponding way realizes this his explicit self without, evoking thereby, in this reduplication of himself, what is in him into vision and into knowledge for his own mind and for that of others. This is the free rationality of man, in which, as all action and knowledge, so also art has its ground and necessary origin. (36)

Another specificity, recognized by both Black and White art critics, is worth mentioning: in traditional Africa, the anonymity of the artist and the keeping of the creator's personality in the background—once the artwork is completed—

has been the rule. However, Rowland Abiodun (2001) sees it as a "presumed anonymity." Yes, there is still a problem identifying individual artists. But he says: "The problem has been exacerbated by the fact that many artists among the Yoruba, for example, do not sign their works in the way artists in other societies have. This has led some Western art historians to the dubious conclusion that African artists merely repeat traditional motifs with no personal creativity or innovation" (18).

Such a situation leads to a great concern that Africans and Africanist scholars in general have been raising. For Senghor, the theorist of Negritude, some anthropologists and arts critics have been claiming that notions of "beauty" and "beautiful" are absent from Negro African languages. It is quite the contrary for Senghor (1956). He explains: "Cependant, on ne saisirait pas l'essence de la literature et de l'art africains en s'imaginant qu'ils sont seulement utilitaires et que le Négro-Africain n'a pas les sens de la *beauté*" [However, we cannot seize the literary and artistic essence in African thinking by thinking that they are only utilitarian and that the Negro African does not have a sense of *beauty*] (208). Ndaw does admit that traditional Africa has not concerned itself in defining norms of pure beauty or beauty in itself. Nevertheless, this fact has not prevented the emergence of an autonomous reflection on the essence of beauty, the nature of artwork, and the meanings of artistic activity.

Thus, the functional aspect does not exclude esthetics, meaning that "clients" and artists' demands could be motivated by a pure esthetic pleasure. Thompson shows that among the Yoruba (Nigeria), there is a long tradition of art critique and that their contemporary art critics are strict and extraordinarily precise in their judgment. He says: "There exists in Subsaharan Africa, locked in the minds of kings, priests, and commoners, a reservoir of artistic criticism. Wherever tapped, this source lends clarity to our understanding of the arts of tropical Africa" (19). In terms of "primitive art," Thompson thinks that "the criteria of primitivism do not apply to the traditional Yoruba" (24), meaning that Westerners must rethink the status of arts and criticism when it comes to African people. Ndaw explains: "Le development de la conscience esthétique négro-Africaine est lié à la mise en evidence de la spécificité de la fonction esthétique, à la recherche, par delà les significations utilitaires, sociales ou religieuses de ce fait qui fait que l'object est beau en lui-même, de ce qui fait que le négro-africain a une conscience de ce beau en dehors de l'idéologie ou de la théorie de son ethnie" [The development of Negro African aesthetic consciousness is connected to the discovery of the specificity of the aesthetic function, research, going beyond utilitarian, social, or religious meanings so that the object is beautiful in-itself, that the Negro African is conscious of such a beauty outside ideologies or theories of ethnicity] (2). However for Ndaw, the most interesting aspect of Thompson's work is his revealing of connections between African and classical Greece esthetic canons: an artistic, complex, and coherent ensemble, which includes many parallels with Western ideals.

Earlier, I mentioned that Africa received outside influence. Africa has, thus, Africanized iconographic and technical elements. One of the results is, for example, the Benin plate whose style was borrowed from illustrations in Portuguese religious books, brought to Africa between the fifteenth and seventeenth centuries. Paula Girshick Ben-Amos (1995) provides ample information on West African groups in present-day Sierra Leone, Guinea Bissau, Western Nigeria, and Zaire being commissioned to make artifacts for Portuguese sailors as well as their nobility. "African-Portuguese" ivories and other art forms were very popular, and are still in existence. Ben-Amos recounts: "Portuguese travelers were readily assimilated into (or perhaps generated) the complex of ideas and motifs associated with the God Olokun, ruler of the sea and provider of earthly wealth. Cast or carved images of Portuguese sailors in sixteenth-century attire appear in a wide variety of contexts—on bracelets, plaques, bells, pendants, masks, tusks, and so on. The image of the Portuguese thus became an integral part of a visual vocabulary of power and wealth" (37).

Therefore, can African artists claim a specificity that incorporates foreign elements, which are now so blended that they have become a unique style? In questioning the past, will committed artists be able to extirpate foreign influences? This is just impossible. To reinforce this impossibility, I shall add that today, more and more, African artists are trained in Europe or the United States as shown in the popular *African Art magazine* from the University of California (UCLA) and seen at the various exhibitions on African arts throughout the world. Even those who are trained in Africa itself undergo the Western influence since curricula offer a combination of African, European, and Asian styles.

I think that only a clear synthesis of the universality and particularity of art can lead to a proper understanding. In terms of African art as a particularity in indefinite ways, it is beautiful in the sense that the subject is derived from human activity. The universality is seen in the "means" rather than in the end product. Human activity is the universal and the end; beauty is simply what all art is intended to be. Again, here is Hegel:

> The philosophic conception of the beautiful, to indicate its true nature at least by anticipation, must contain, reconciled within it, the two extremes which have been mentioned, by combining metaphysical universality with the determinateness of real particularity. Only thus is it apprehended in its truth, in its real explicit nature. It is then fertile out of its own resources, in contrast to the barrenness of one-sided reflection. For it has in accordance with its own conception to develop into a totality of attributes, while the conception itself as well as its detailed exposition contains the necessity of it particulars, as also of their progress and transition one into another. On the other hand, again, these particulars, to which the transition is made, carry in themselves the universality and essentiality of the conception of which we have so far been treating lack both these qualities, and for this reason it is only the complete conception of which we have just spoken that can lead to substantive necessary, an self-complete determinations. (26)

For Hegel, art is a figurative expression of the spirit; the intelligible element in which the sensitive element finds itself and the universal unites with the singular. He says: "Spirit is *Artist*" (708). Thus art is the concrete and sensitive incarnation of the Idea; it is the synthesis of the idea and the form. Therefore, art is an important moment in the elevation of humans towards Absolute knowledge. In his Study of Hegel's *Aesthetics*, G. I. Gouliane (1970) explains that "L'art exige une liberté de création parfaite, une fantaisie illimitée, les moyens de varier les formes à l'infini" [Art demands a total freedom of creation, a bondless imagination, and means to alter forms ad infinitum] (277).

Indeed, for Hegel human beings express their freedom in art. They are not subjected to any rule and do not slavishly imitate nature. On the contrary, with an unlimited imagination in their creations, they recreate and reinvent nature. Therefore, art is the stamp of freedom. For Hegel—and this is quite clear—the work of art is superior to nature because it is the expression of the spirit. He says: "The work of art stands higher than any natural product that has not made his journey through the spirit" (29). Thus art is higher in value than any product of nature because it is a product of the spirit.

For Hegel, one cannot consider just any form of art. There is a minor art, which is only a pleasant pastime. Hegel's analyses help him elaborate more his fundamental thesis: "The work of art attains the appearance of life only on its surface. A true work of art is only so because, originating from the spirit, it now belongs to the territory of the spirit; it has received the baptism of the spiritual and sets forth only what has been formed in harmony with the spirit" (29).

Hegel's efforts to establish a scientific theory of art and the beautiful are also part of his criticism of empiricist aesthetics. In Gouliane's words "Le connaisseur apporte une idée précieuse voire indispensable, mais l'érudition (qui est une accumulation de faits et de connaissances) ne saurait remplacer l'esthétique" [The connoisseur offers a precious and indispensible contribution but erudition (an accumulation of facts and knowledge could not replace Aesthetics] (278). Since everyone likes to be equipped with the most essential physical fact—just as a cultured person needs to have some acquaintance with art—Hegel offers the following requirement: "Every work of art belongs to its time, its own people, its own environment, and depends on particular historical and other ideas and purposes; consequently, scholarship in the field of art demands a vast wealth of historical, and indeed very detailed, facts, since the individual nature of the work of art is related to something individual and necessarily requires detailed knowledge for its understanding and explanation" (14).

For Sigmund Freud (1961), the love of beauty seems a perfect example of an impulse inhibited in its aims. He says: "Happiness, in the reduced sense in which we recognize it as possible, is a problem of the economics of the individual's libido. It is a question of how much real satisfaction [one] (he) is led to make himself independent of it, and finally, how much strength he feels he has for altering the world to suit his wishes. In this, his psychical constitution will play a decisive part, irrespectively of the external circumstances" (30).

Therefore, I see two approaches: if African art is studied from an ethnophilosophical point of view, it will eternize in the selection of what is specific and what is not; if studied from an esthetic point of view, Negro African art will conform—to a great extent—to the hypostasis of individual exigencies as in the Freudian theory of art and aesthetic pleasure.

Of African Languages

Ideological factors have always shrouded linguistics in Africa. European imperialism has equated languages and their families with races. African languages and their speakers have been seen as less developed, and therefore primitive. George Tucker Childs (2003) explains:

> Non-European languages were not surprisingly considered to be more primitive, and thus lower on an evolutionary scale, than those displaying grammatical features of the languages of the European analysts. This reasoning resulted in the "racist" 'Hamitic' concept, which wrongly brought physical type and cultural traits such as pastoralism into linguistic classification. [Consequently], languages such as Fula, Maasai, Somali, and Nama were grouped together in a group called "Hamitic" and were said to have varying amount of "Negro admixture" and belong to a superior Caucasoid racial type. (35)

The theory of the Hamites often comes up whenever we are dealing with African properties, and postulates a White or semi-White race in Africa. They would have triggered all major accomplishments, including empire building in Black Africa. Diop (1988), among other Africanist scholars, has refuted such a theory as having no serious or scientific basis. His point is that if there were such people, their birthplace, languages, the migration routes they have followed, the counties of regions they have settled, the form of civilization they may have left, would have been known yet. They are not unless, of course, generations of Africans have become amnesiac throughout history.

Today, it has been made clear that Negro African languages, which present themselves as universal, do indeed show the existence of universal categories proper to all world languages, hence the labeling of "languages." As with all world languages, African ones are the product of human institutions, thus assuming the fundamental function of communication among humans. Researchers have proposed hypotheses on the languages' genesis, relationships and classifications in broad linguistic families. To such various levels of scholarships, one can connect the following names: Karl Meinhof, Maurice Delafosse, Diedrich Westermann, Diop, Pathé Diagne, Aurélien Sauvageot, Joseph Greenberg, Frank Boas, and many others. However, André Martinet (1982) has especially established the unity of human languages and the integral insertion of Negro African ones into a general schema:

> A language is an instrument of communication in virtue of which human experience is analyzed differently in each given community into units, the monemes, each endowed with a semantic content and a phonic expression. The phonic expression is articulated in its turn into distinctive and successive units. These are the phonemes, of limited number in each language, their nature and mutual relations varying from one language to another (29).

This definition, together with the preceding considerations, shows the basis common to all languages and at the same time, it signals their distinction and particularities. In relation to human experience, Diop says, "in fact, language, even non-written, must be considered a crystallization of enigmas belonging to a people and more or less difficult to decipher. Language necessarily carries the traces of a people's past" (201-2). Today, it is estimated that there are over 2500 languages spoken on the African continent, with possibly as many as 8000 dialects. Whatever the number, Bern Heine and Derek Nurse (2000) add that it will not be a fixed one, "as some languages are still being 'discovered,' while others with few speakers are being eliminated; If we believe this figure, then it represents nearly one-third of the world's languages" (1).

As for the specificities of African languages—in form or in structure—they do no reside in the so-called poverty of African languages. A language cannot be judged as being poor in relation to a well-determined civilization, which it expresses. Language can be judged as such only when it refers to a standard civilization with an ethnocentric background. The specificities are not in the opposite thesis of wealthy African languages. Maquet puts in the following terms:

> However, the often-repeated affirmation of wealthy African languages seems to verify itself in many cases. This wealth reveals itself in the vocabulary. Westermann mentions that the adjective "big" can be translated in 183 words in Nupe and 311 words in Hausa languages. As Mr. Senghor notes: "There are ten, sometimes twenty words to name an object, depending on its form, weight, volume, and color; there are many words to express an action depending on its uniqueness or multiplicity, weakness, intensity, or beginning or end. (30)

Kwame A. Appiah (1992) views the lack of written tradition in much of Black Africa as a handicap to a real "philosophy": Appiah explains that "The lack of writing has left nothing more to Africa than an oral folk philosophy. This oral folkloric philosophy does not exhibit that quality of philosophic reasoning. [Moreover], it is unable to treat critical activity as disinterested" (91). Even if it is so, the use of 'folk' tends to have negative connotations and above all, does not do justice to the richness and beauty of verbal art productions. Saying that African thinkers are "interested" (i.e., deal with the concrete) makes little more sense than saying that Western philosophers are "disinterested" (i.e., deal with abstraction). Both are making the same use of theory to transcend phenomena and understand the world.

Pierre Alexandre's (1972) reaction—made twenty-five years ago—seems to anticipate this way of thinking when he says:

> It seems probable that in civilizations whose culture is exclusively or primarily oral, the active vocabulary (one which is actually used or spoken as opposed to a vocabulary, which is merely understood. The passive vocabulary is always larger than the active vocabulary where literacy is widespread) which each person has at his command is larger—precisely because of the lack of graphic memory aids—than it is in a civilization which makes extensive use of writing. (33)

In terms of African languages being too concrete and fundamentally lacking ways to express abstract ideas, Alexandre has this to say: "A language may be more analytical in some spheres, more synthetic in others. The global wealth of expression may well be the same for all languages. The vocabulary which people possess, given equal capacity of the speakers, is practically identical from one language to another" (34).

Thus, a language does not solely define itself by its oral form. Because, even though the bulk of African languages are oral, one cannot solely define them by their oral form; one can always add a written form as it is today. Many African countries have used Latin alphabet to write their languages. That is why I maintain that oral and written forms complement each other and most likely, African languages find in their oral form that which the absence of writing has deprived them of.

For the Cameroonian philosopher Ebenezer Njoh-Mouelle (1975), concreteness is a great specificity of African languages. He says: "Il me semble au contraire que le penseur African traditional évolue au sein même de l'Etre et que les mots et les signes qu'il utilise coincident avec le signifié lui-même. Je dirais, sans crainte de me tromper, que pour les langues africaines et dans leur usage traditional, les mots sont les choses" [On the contrary, it seems to me that traditional African thinkers evolve within the Being and that the words and signs they use coincide with the signified itself. I would state with certainty that for African languages, in their traditional usage, words are things] (32). After providing examples from his native Douala languages, Njoh-Mouelle adds:

> Cette remarque me paraît d'autant plus importante que si les mots sont des réalités, on comprend aisément que l'abstraction recherchée comme la marque par excellence de toute démarche philosophique ne soit pas particulièrement nécessaire aux langues africaines. Ici, au lieu de manipuler pour ainsi dire, les abstractions, on manipule les réalités concrètes et les mots eux-mêmes sont de telles réalités fortement solidaires des significations qu'ils sont chargés de vehiculer [This remark seems all the more important since words are realities; one can easily understand that the abstract that is sought after—as a token par excellence of any philosophical process—is not particularly necessary for African languages. Here, instead of handling abstractions so to speak, we handle con-

crete realities, and words themselves are realities very strongly linked to the meanings that they are supposed to convey]. (33)

If the objective criteria for specifying Negro African languages are not in the above, then one must look somewhere else. At this level, the answer becomes technical and I do not propose here to enter into the jargon and technical details of the articulary phonetics. I am going to offer a few examples of those linguistic features unique to Africa or rarely found elsewhere.

The most striking of them is perhaps the use of tone-systems. In many languages of Black Africa, there are two or three distinct levels of pitch and these are used to determine meaning. For Alexandre, the question of tones deserves a special attention because they are significant in African languages. He explains, "The musical pitch of one syllable is as important to the meaning of the message as the timber of the vowels or the articulation of the consonants" (36). Childs explains, "in African languages, every syllable or mora has its own tone, and the inventory will consist of two level tones, a high and a low, and one or two contour tones, a rise and/or fall" (76). His study shows that African tones "are perhaps the most challenging and fascinating phonological phenomenon of all" (76). Thus, in most Negro African languages, the musical height is pertinent or in other words, intervenes in the distinction of meanings of messages. It is impossible to speak or to communicate without respecting the tones.

Phonetically and phonologically, we should point out what Alexandre calls an "African monopoly": the cliks. Technically, Heine and Nurse explain them as being "A multiply articulated sound produced by forming one closure in the front of the mouth with the lips or tongue in front and another in the back of the mouth with the tongue dorsum. The air pocket trapped between the two closures is expanding by drawing the tongue body downward and backward while maintaining both closures, and the front closure is then released to produce the characteristic click burst as air rushes into the mouth ('the influx')" (150).

Outside Khoisan, clicks are known to occur only in South African Bantu languages such as Zulu, Xhosa, Southern Sotho, Yeyi, and in small isolated pockets in Tanzania. To these languages, one can add the Cushitic language Dahalo. The Johannesburg native international singer Miriam Makeba—better known as Mama Africa—has popularized clicks with her "Click Song" (1994). According to Alexander, clicks are used as phonemic consonants, which serve to form syllables.

In Africa, one can also notice prenazalized consonants and syllables. For Childs, "Prenazalized segments are relatively uncommon in languages of the world; they are richly distributed in the languages of Sub-Saharan Africa" (62). Thus, characteristic of many African languages is the sequence of nasal sound (*n*- or *m*-) plus a voice stop such as -*b* or -*d*, or a guttural like—*g*. The combined sounds *mb*-, *nd*-, *nk*- or *ng* are frequent and characteristic as in the names 'Nkrumah,' 'Nzerekore,' or 'ngaounde' among others. A further distinguishing feature of these languages is the fact that syllables are usually "open," that is they end on a vowel, not a consonant. To this list, one could add the doubling of the root of a vocable or part of its root as a very common trait, having a stylistic, semantic or grammatical function. In Hausa, we have 'mùùni' (ugliness) and 'mummùùnàà' (ugly).

From a sociological stand, African languages are characterized by a near lack of written form. Does such a rarity justify the internationally popular Malian writer Amadou Hampâté Bâ's analysis? This African anthropologist thinks,

> Dans les civilizations orales la parole engage l'homme, la parole est l'homme. D'où le respect profond des récits traditionnels légués par le passé, dont il est permis d'embellir la forme ou la tournure poétique, mais dont la trame reste immuable à travers les siècles, véhiculée par une mémoire prodigieuse qui est la charastéristique même des peoples à tradition orale. Dans la civilization moderne, le papier s'est substitué à la parole. C'est lui qui engage l'homme [In oral tradition civilizations, words engage human beings; words equal humans; hence, the profound respect given to traditional stories inherited from the past. Their poetic form or tournure can be embellished but the structure remains unchanged throughout the centuries because they are conveyed by a phenomenal memory, which represents the very characteristic of oral tradition societies. In our modern civilization, paper has replaced the word. It is now what engages human beings]. (75)

For Alexandre, "En termes plus simples, il y a de fortes chances qu'on trouve de meilleurs causeurs là où il n'y a pas, ou guère, d'écrivains et de lecteurs" [In simpler terms, there is a strong chance that one finds the best conversationalists where there are no writers and readers at all] (45).

Such are some of the characteristics proper to Negro African languages we have found. Next to elements common to all these languages, there are traits that can only be found in linguistic groups or families and whose frequency is quite striking. Therefore, they can be interpreted as marks of specificity, particularly when we keep in mind the possible objectivity of the theses of an Ancient Egyptian origin, common to all African languages. In Janheinz Jahn's (1994) words: "It would be wrong to ask why they [Black Africans] did not 'invent' writing, for firstly, our [European American] writing probably was invented by Africans in Egypt and then developed further by Phoenicians; and secondly, various scripts were constantly invented south of the Sahara also, some of which even came into limited use: the writing of the Vai, which, like the Egyptian, was a picture writing, the Nsibidi, a syllabic script of an Efic secret society, and others as well" (186).

Chapter Five

From the Concept of Labor to the Labor of Concept

The concept of labor is undoubtedly the best way to apprehend Hegel's thought in its totality. Indeed, the Hegelian system—and Marxist analysis—rests entirely on the meaning that they give to labor. Hegel does not change or modify at all the meaning of labor once he has forged the concept. It becomes one of the pillars of his philosophical vision. In his *Reason and Revolution* (1963), Herbert Marcuse stresses the fact: "The concept of labor is not peripheral in Hegel's system, but is the central notion through which he conceives the development of society" (78).

For Hegel, labor is the first sign of human responsibility. At the same time, it turns human beings into not just simple creators but God-like ones. Therefore, human beings free themselves from divine control and become masters of their own destiny, thus, creating culture and making history. The practical and historical process is founded in labor. This seems to be the fundamental moment when the Spirit chooses to emerge in-itself and, through the purifying bath of social and historic substance, heads toward the Absolute.

Labor, Production, and Human Self-Production

For human beings, anything that is not themselves is their others. Individuals are in immediate relation with others. To maintain themselves, to be, individuals are compelled to consume and consume others. This world is their other. The world or nature is "human beings' non-organic part." Human beings seize the world and make it their organs. They make organs or instruments to appropriate the world. Individuals or human beings can only be conceived in their indissoluble connection with the world. Humans are parts or elements of the totality that is universal life; they are totally engaged in nature's movement. That is why, for Hegel, the individual is subjected to "the infinity of difference."

The relation between the spirit and nature is not one of dependency. Indeed, consciousness or the spirit, by penetrating and transforming nature, elevates it and gives it life and a true existence. The spirit shapes nature to give it a human face. The spirit actualizes itself, becomes alive, and reveals itself in and by labor.

Thus Hegel, has acquired the idea that the relation between human beings and nature is not a passive or contemplative one but rather, a relation of transformation and action. The concept of labor is a form of activity: it is action. Its symbol is iron in general; iron is the very expression of a vital activity. Anything that is activity or display of effort is a form of labor. Memory is already an act of labor in the sense that it allows human beings to develop the capability to perceive themselves in time. The permanent consciousness of the past, present, and future is indispensible to the human collectivity.

Labor is overall non-production of material but production of human beings or themselves. Human beings must conquer everything: they are only potentialities which are powers to conquer themselves in the process. The definition of human essence for Hegel is the same as his conception of the spirit itself, which is its own work. There is no difference between what human beings do and what they are. Labor is, therefore, production and human beings' self-production. Marx echoes Hegel:

> It is just in his work upon the objective world, therefore, that man really proves himself to be a *species-being*. This production is his active species-life. Through this production, nature appears as *his* work and his reality. The object of labor is, therefore, the *objectification of man's species-life*: for he duplicates himself not only, as in consciousness, intellectually, but also actively, in reality, and therefore, he sees himself in a world that he has created. In tearing away from man the object of his production, therefore estranged labor tears from him his species-life, his real objectivity as a member of the species, and transforms his advantage over animals into the disadvantage that his inorganic body, nature, is taken away from him. (69)

This excludes the concept of an unchanging nature. The formation of the process of human nature happens in history. Thus, there is no difference between human beings' essence and their acts; there is no closed inferiority; everything is both internal and external. In the cultural process, humans become aware of what they are. There are spirits and potentialities, but these potentialities are only in and by the actions that show them. Even if human beings depend on nature, their work is what they make of nature, and they are conscious of it.

Hegel opposes the deification of nature and the current conception according to which human beings' production would be minimal. For him, the transformation is a fundamental activity. What makes human beings' dignity is not their nature or spiritual essence, but their production of objects, which is the production of their selves. Two myths, chosen by Hegel in his *Philosophy of Religion* explain the essence of labor: (1) the myth of Prometheus: Prometheus steals fire from the Gods to give it to humanity, thereby becoming humankind's hero. His gesture marks the transformation of nature and the beginning of history; (2) the myth of the fall: it is the split between divinity and humanity. The condemnation of the fall on earth is in fact the affirmation of humanity.

The Myth of the Fall: Apparition of the Labor Moment

Genesis 2 and 3 tell the story of Adam and Eve:

> God fashions a man from the dust and blowing life into his nostrils. God plants a garden (the Garden of Eden) and sets the man there, "to work it and watch over it," permitting him to eat of all the trees in the garden except the Tree of Knowledge of Good and Evil, "for on the day you eat of it you shall surely die." God had already created the animals. When Adam tries to find a helpmate, none of the animals are satisfactory, and so God causes the man to sleep, and creates a woman from his rib. The man names her "Woman," "for this one was taken from a man." *Genesis 3* introduces the Serpent, "slier than every beast of the field." The serpent tempts the woman to eat from the tree of knowledge, telling her that it will make her more like God and it will not lead to death. She succumbs, and gives the fruit to the man, who eats also, "and the eyes of the two of them were opened." God then curses Adam and Eve with hard labor and with pain in childbirth, and banishes them from his garden. (9-11)

By deliberately choosing to eat of the forbidden fruit, human beings have freed themselves from the condition of natural consciousness to reach the knowledge of good and evil. Therefore, they now reveal themselves as spirits because to know good and evil means to have the freedom to posit them; and spirit is freedom.

Paradise, the immediate and harmonious unity between human beings and good, is in fact a state of naturalness, a primitive state, a state of insouciance, innocence, unconsciousness, irresponsibility, and childhood—a child cannot know freedom. With the fall, human beings become spirits. The spirit is in fact free and what it is must be by itself. Freedom is not a definitive possession but, on the contrary, it is a negation, negativity, and therefore cannot be given: it is a development that is permanently conquering itself.

Human beings—for having violated the prohibition—are chastised and driven out of paradise. God says: "Cursed be the ground for thy sake, in sorrow shalt thou eat what it brings forth to thee; thorns and thistles shall it bear to thee, and thou shalt eat the herb of the field. In the sweat of thy face, shalt thou eat thou bread, and thou shalt return unto the ground, for out of it wast thou taken;

for dust thou art, and unto dust shalt thou return" (202). To be driven out of paradise is thus a severe punishment brought up by a lack of respect for the law.

This capital moment marks the separation of human beings from both nature's and divinity's control. It is the beginning of human culture for the fall is the apparition of the labor moment. Nature becomes a matter submitted to human activities. The feeling of insecurity human beings discover in nakedness is the birth of humans' *prise de conscience* as free and responsible beings. The fall marks the moment of the passage from in-itself to for-itself. Being free from their state of creatures has permitted human beings to become creators themselves. Nature itself is only a mean, a point of departure, and a matter to shape, which allow the spirit to find itself back.

In labor, human beings destroy and negate the biologic nature on which they depend. The appropriation of human culture supposes a division or a split. However, labor is not a sentence—by the sweat of thy brow shalt thy eat bread—but an instrument of human liberation *vis à vis* themselves, the others. There is no punishment; on the contrary, it is simply the consecration of human nature, which is to be free. Human beings, as we have seen, are not dust. By pronouncing the fall of humankind, God in fact, enounces its sublimity. Hegel writes: "The serpent says that Adam will become like God, and God confirms the truth of this, and adds his testimony that it is this knowledge, which constitutes likeness to God" (202). Thus, human beings have acquired the divine power to be creators and no longer simple creatures.

Therefore, human destiny is a noble and elevated one. In fact, Hegel writes: "The fact that man regarded from the natural side is also free, is involved in his nature, and is not to be considered as in itself punishment. The sorrow of the natural life is essentially connected with the greatness of the character and destiny of man" (203). Labor thus allows human beings to distinguish themselves among living beings. With labor, they master nature for their needs, ideals, and purposes. While animals satisfy their needs in nature, human beings manifest their freedom by working. Therefore, the primitive harmony is only naïve consciousness and animal life. Human beings must not dwell in naturalness and the rupture or the fall is the point of departure for the humanization of nature and the affirmation of humans. Hegel writes that in fact: "Man is exalted above all else in the whole creation. He is something which knows, perceives, and thinks. He is thus the image of God in a sense quite other than that in which the same is true of the world" (198-99).

The fall or rupture with God leads human beings to no longer expect from him the elements that would allow them to fully realize themselves. Hegel writes that from that moment onward, "It [consciousness] has thus itself expressed in an abstract way the immediate unity of thought and existence, of abstract Essential Reality and Self; and when it has expressed the primal principle of "Light" in a purer form, viz. as unity of extension and existence" (802).

This situation of no return leads human beings—themselves, the finite beings—to go all the way to their proper realization, to be infinite, and to reconcile with the divine.

The Myth of Prometheus

The myth of Prometheus who has stolen fire from the God to give it to humans, deals with the beginning of human civilization and destiny. Benjamin Jowett (1996) offers a version of the myth:

> Once upon a time there were gods only, and no mortal creatures. But when the time came that these also should be created, the gods fashioned them out of earth and fire and various mixtures of both elements in the interior of the earth; and when they were about to bring them into the light of day, they ordered Prometheus and Epimetheus to equip them, and to distribute to them severally their proper qualities. Thus did Epimetheus, who, not being very wise, forgot that he had distributed among the brute animals all the qualities, which he had to give-and when he came to man, who was still unprovided [while] other animals were suitably furnished, but that man alone was naked and shoeless, and had neither bed nor arms of defense. The power of Prometheus did not extend to entering into the citadel of heaven, where Zeus dwelt, who moreover had terrible sentinels; but he did enter by stealth into the common workshop of Athena and Hephaestus . . . and carried off Hephaestus' art of working by fire, and also the art of Athena, and gave them to man. And in this way man was supplied with the means of life. (320-28 d)

Here again, the Gods' punishment is severe. For his crime, "Prometheus is chained to the Caucus, and a vulture constantly gnaws at his liver, which always grows again—a pain, which never ceases" (237). This myth thus expresses human beings' insatiable needs. Moreover, for Hegel, Prometheus is the inventor of the first industrial technique. This gift of fire is a capital one. Hegel says: "Prometheus is the power of Nature, but he is also the benefactor of men, for he taught them the first arts. He brought down fire from heaven for them; the power to kindle fire already implies a certain amount of civilization; it means that man has already got beyond his primitive barbarism" (236).

The kindling of fire is also a victory over the fear of a natural element; now it is rather used to frighten. Therefore, it is a first victory over nature and oneself. Human beings, using fire to transform nature for the satisfaction of their needs, accomplish their first natural act. For Hegel, culture begins with fire and iron. Therefore, Prometheus is the father of human society. This myth signifies the permanent necessity for human beings to work and satisfy their vital needs. Hegel writes: "In the mere satisfaction of [humans' natural wants], there is never any sense of satiety; on the contrary, the need is always growing and care is ever new" (237).

Labor as a medium-term, meaning a mediation between human beings and nature, consciousness, and other—by allowing the possibility of a cultural and historical world—no longer leads to the unity of the dismal and lifeless subject-object. On the contrary, by allowing the possibility of a cultural and historical world, it leads to a unity in which particularities, singularities, oppositions, and duality reside. Labor is indeed the means by which human beings and nature develop an intimate liaison in a tight relation while the duality human beings/nature and consciousness/being continue to exist. The medium term plays an essential role. Hegel writes: "This negative mediating agency, this activity giving shape and form, is at the same time the individual existence the pure self-existence of that consciousness" (238). For Hegel, the affirmation and realization of humanity suppose and demand this fundamental relation between human beings and nature. This relation, which expresses and incarnates itself in labor, is not a simple relation; on the contrary, it is a difficult and complex one that implies a true split.

Human beings leave their primitive and naïve life and harmony and their in-itself to integrate themselves into the universe and transform it. Human beings become revolutionaries and revolutionize the world. However, because of the inevitable identity between revolutionary and revolutionized, there exists in revolutionized human beings a radical self-revolution and self-transformation. Consciousness transforms itself, ceases to be theoretical, and becomes practical; henceforth, pure reflection is not a goal in itself and neither is knowledge.

Consciousness reaches its perfect realization only in and by the conquest and possession of nature, and this, thanks to human labor. Hegel writes: "L'idée pratique est supérieure à celle de la connaissance car elle a non seulement la dignité du général, mais celle du réel par excellence [A practical idea is superior to the one of knowledge because, not only it possesses the dignity of the general but also the dignity of the real per excellence] (54).

The result of such activity is that all splits, all oppositions, all dualism are superseded in the sense that supersession does not mean a simple negation but a negation/conservation as in *Aufhebung*. The pure ego is true freedom transcending all natural determinations; however, the difference is that, from now on, as Hegel puts it, there is no more totally empty gap, without relation, separating the absolute singularity and the totality of determinates.

A pure consciousness that enjoys an Absolute freedom sanctions the separation of thought and being. On the moral level, this translates into crime and, in the *Phenomenology*, it leads to stoicism. Such a constantly dissatisfied consciousness is an unhappy one. It is a consciousness that endures a perpetual drama, which consumes it. That is why a theoretical consciousness calls for a practical one: the unity of thought and being, which is the foundation of absolute knowledge. The practical and effective activity resides in its foundation, in the reconciliation of thought with being and spirit with the world. In this sense, Jean Hyppolyte (1969) writes: "Thought and life are no longer to be separate domains, where life always outstrips thought and thought never comprehends life.

The two terms are to be identified so that life is conceptualized as life and thought breaks with its traditional form in order to grasp and express life itself" (4). There is no more duality between the essence and its phenomena, which are now identical. In the historical reality, necessity becomes inseparable from the apparent contingency.

Labor as Universal

Labor division, resulting from the very exigencies of the economic organization of life, means that workers not only work to satisfy their own needs but also those of the whole global society. Labor ceases to be a particular act and becomes a universal one. Hegel writes:

> The labor of the individual for his own wants is just as much a satisfaction of those of others as of himself, and the satisfaction of his own he attains only by the labor of others. As the individual in his own particular work *ipso facto* accomplishes unconsciously a universal work, so again he also performs the universal task as his conscious object, The whole becomes in its entirety his work, for which he sacrifices himself, and precisely by that means receives back his own self from it. (377)

Economic life thus transcends the individual needs that have given it birth. It allows the individual to come out of isolation. The individual is put in contact with other individuals. Therefore, individuals become more and more socialized and, from then onwards, social relations happen at a wider and more global dimension. Thus, individuals are not alone and isolated and human life is not fragmented or parceled out. On the contrary, human beings in their lives are in touch and communicate with each other. Such relations are determinant in fact since individuals—to reach a perfect and indispensible unity—feel the needs of other individuals with whom they maintain social relations.

For humans, the desire to satisfy their biological needs (to eat, drink etc.), which is common to all animals, is not enough. Humans desire other humans. They desire to be recognized by other humans to finally establish a perfect unity with their lives. This crucial point that Hegel makes stresses a difference and a superiority of human beings over animals. Beasts confound themselves totally and directly with their vital activity. Human beings require more. In Marx's words: "The animal is immediately one with *its life activity*. It does not distinguish itself from it. It is its life-activity. Man makes his life activity itself the object of his will and of his consciousness. He has conscious life activity" (68). Hegel's position is also very familiar to Africans: it is at the heart of their social beliefs and has become a common saying on the continent. Wolof people say: "Nit nitay garabam" [a human being's medicine is another human being].

The desire that a consciousness feels for another and the ensuing movement become true around labor.

The Hegelian Master-Slave Dialectic

This concept has shed a lot of ink among thinkers around the world since Hegel and seems to have been revived as authors such as Nick Nesbitt's *Universal Emancipation: the Haitian Revolution and the Radical Enlightenment* (2008) and Susan Buck-Morss's *Hegel Haiti, and Universal Story* (2009), are proving that the Haitian Revolution of 1804 has inspired Hegel to develop such a concept. Frederic L. Luqueer's *Hegel as Educator* (1896), John Russon's *Reading Hegel's Phenomenology* (2004), and Allen Speight's *The Philosophy of Hegel* (2008) provide explanations of the famous slave-master dialectic but have not added anything new. Alexandre Kojève's *Introduction to the Reading of Hegel* (1980) has made the concept more popular and is credited to have revived it at a time when "[Hegel] seems no longer of living significance." It is then wise to hear the full concept from Hegel himself:

> The master is the consciousness that exists *for itself*; but no longer merely the general notion of existence for self. Rather, it is a consciousness existing on its own account, which is mediated with itself through another consciousness, i.e. through another whose very nature implies that it is bound up with an independent being or with thinghood in general. The master brings himself into relation to both these moments, to a thing as such, the object of desire, and to the consciousness whose essential character is thinghood. And since the master, is (*a*) *qua* notion of self-consciousness, an immediate relation of self-existence, but (*b*) is now moreover at the same time mediation, or a being-for-itself, which is for itself only through the other—he [the master] stands in relation (*a*) immediately to both (*b*) mediately to each through the other. The master relates himself to the bondsman mediately through independent existence, for that is precisely what keeps the bondsman in thrall; it is his chain, from which he could not in the struggle get away, and for that reason he proves himself to be dependent, to have his independence in the shape of thinghood. The master, however, is the power controlling this state of existence, for he has shown in the struggle that he holds it to be merely something negative. Since he is the power dominating existence, while this existence again is the power controlling the other [the bondsman], the master holds, *par consequence*, this other in subordination. In the same way the master relates himself to the thing mediately through the bondsman. The bondsman being a self-consciousness in the broad sense, also takes up a negative attitude to things and cancels them; but the thing is, at the same time, independent for him, and, in consequence, he cannot, with all his negating, get so far as to annihilate it outright and be done with it; that is to say, he merely works on it. To the master on the other hand, by means of this mediating process, belongs the immediate relation, in the sense of the pure negation of it, in other words he gets the enjoyment. What mere desire did not attain, he now succeeds in attaining, viz. to have done with the thing, and find

satisfaction in enjoyment. Desire alone did not get the length of this, because of the independence of the thing. The master, however, who has interposed the bondsman between it and himself, thereby relates himself merely to the dependence of the thing, and enjoys it without qualification and without reserve. The aspect of its independence he leaves to the bondsman, who labors upon it. (234-36)

Desire

Hegel presents human beings as immersed in nature where they belong. Their consciousness is not pure consciousness but it is a consciousness immersed in reality. Consciousness then becomes aware of itself with action and becomes a practical consciousness that appropriates things. The sensitive world appears as the other they want to assimilate: such is Desire.

Differently form the Cartesian "I," the Hegelian "I" is characterized by dissatisfaction, shortage, and need. Thus, in its relation with the world, the "I" expresses and shows its desire. Basically, desire aims at the unity of "I" and the world, subjectivity, and objectivity. Therefore, the world is the non-truth, the loss of self or "I," and thus, to exist the "I" must consume or suppress it.

However, there are two moments in Desire: the desire of the world and the desire of the other. The desire of the world, the need is satisfied in creative labor: the "I" then takes the world as the self-other that must be suppressed in order to maintain himself as ego. The other, the world, is negativity; to exist, consciousness must transform the real. However, the "I" does not content itself with the satisfaction of such a desire, which establishes and accepts his objective existence. More fundamentally, the "I" wants to find his self-conscious being. And this is possible only when the initially primitive desire of an object changes itself into the desire of desire. The "I" is life and only life is its objective. The essential Desire thus is the desire of the other, the desire to be recognized by the other as a consciousness, as life. Hegel says:

> The unity of self-consciousness with itself] must become essential to self-consciousness, i.e. self-consciousness is *Desire* in general. Consciousness, as self-consciousness, henceforth has a double object: one is the immediate object that of sense-certainty and perception, which however for self-consciousness has the character of a *negative*; and the second, viz. *itself*, which is the true *essence*, and is present in the first instance only as opposed to the first object. In this sphere, self-consciousness exhibits itself as the movement in which this antithesis is removed, and the identity of itself becomes explicit for it. (105)

Such recognition of the "I" by another "I" already exists in love. Indeed in his youthful writings, Hegel sees love as having a unifying power. He says: "In [love], the opposite aspects of the human mind are originally united—subjectivity and objectivity; animal and rational nature; individuality and universality; motive and law; the psychological and ethical; realistic and idealistic, volitional and intellectual powers of man's soul" (12). The young Hegel thinks that the recognition one finds in love is the most unifying one can possibly conceive. In love, the two partners want to each be loved and recognized as a universal value in their particularity. Such universal recognition of singularity is satisfaction and happiness.

However, in the *Phenomenology*, Hegel abandons such a position. He says: "The life of God and divine intelligence, then, can, if we like, be spoken of as love disporting with itself; but this idea falls into edification, and even sinks into insipidity, if it lacks the seriousness, the suffering, the patience, and the labor of the negative" (81). Love recognition is no longer the greatest element. Indeed, the character of the love between two individuals is essentially private. Even if an individual is loved, he or she can only be loved by a limited number of persons. Therefore, love recognition cannot be a universal one. Love itself lacks seriousness because, in love, there is no life risk while a true recognition, one with a true value, involves life risking. Hyppolite explains:

> For this reason, the encounter between self-consciousness appears in the *Phenomenology* as a struggle between them for recognition. Desire is less the desire that characterizes love than that of one desiring consciousness from the virile recognition of another desiring consciousness. The movement of recognition, thus, will manifest itself through the opposition between self-consciousnesses. Each consciousness, indeed, will have to show itself as it is to be, that is, as raised above life, which conditions it and by which it is still imprisoned. (164)

The limit of love recognition resides in the fact that the loved being is recognized as universal value and not the action or the deed accomplished by the loved individual. We love human beings not because of what they do but because of what they are. Therefore, in the end love recognition represents only a secondary manifestation of recognition. For Hegel, only struggle and labor—born out of the Desire of "I" to be recognized by another "I" as consciousness and life value—can create realities or specifically human deeds. Struggle and labor, born out of the desire of recognition among humans, trigger the springing of a technical, social, and political world.

The Death Struggle

The recognition of the other first supposes a conflict. This is what highly distinguishes human beings from animals. While animals are constantly guided by their self-preservation instinct, human beings, in order to preserve the meaning and plenitude of life, must exhibit and run the risk of losing it in this implacable struggle to be recognized by other human beings. Thus, human beings rise above simple and natural determinations and empirical solicitations, and affirm themselves as different from animals: human beings are superior to animals.

In this crucial struggle between the two consciousnesses, it so happens that, in the end, one takes the risk of coming close to death without stopping while the other starts trembling and lowering its weapons. In Hegel's words: "For this consciousness was not in peril and fear of this element or that, nor for this and that moment of time, it was afraid of its entire being; it felt the fear of death, the sovereign master. It has been in that experience melted to its inmost soul, has trembled throughout its every fiber, and all that was fixed and steadfast has quaked within it" (237). The victorious fighter, whose consciousness has recognized itself during the struggle and has become self-consciousness, becomes the Master. The other fighter, defeated by the inability to break of nature and be able to recognize self-consciousness in the other, automatically becomes the slave and is subjected to the master's laws. Kojève's Marxist lenses explain Hegel's point:

> The Master forces the Slave to work. And by working, the Slave becomes master of nature. Now, he became the Master's slave only because—in the beginning—he was a slave of Nature, joining with it subordinating himself to its law by accepting the instinct of preservation. In becoming master of nature by work, then, the Slave frees himself from his own nature, from his own instinct that tied him to Nature and made him the Master's Slave. Therefore, by freeing the Slave from Nature, work frees him from himself as well, from his Slave's nature: it frees him from the Master. In the raw, natural, given World, the Slave is slave of the Master. In the technical world transformed by his work, he rules—or, at least, will one day rule—as absolute Master. And this Mastery that arises from work, from the progressive transformation of the given World and of man given in this World, will be an entirely different thing from the "immediate" Mastery of the Master. The future and history hence belong to the warlike Master, who either dies or preserves himself indefinitely in identity to himself, but to the working slave. The Slave, in transforming the given world by his work, transcends the given and what is given by that given in himself, and also goes beyond the Master who is tied to the given which, not working, he leaves intact. If the fear of death, incarnated for the Slave in the person of the warlike Master, is the *sine qua non* of historical progress, it is solely the Slave's work that realizes and perfects it. (23)

At this point, a new situation creates itself. From now on, the masters have slaves who must accomplish all the labors for them at their disposal. They are now intermediaries between masters and nature. In such a situation, masters no longer need to be effective with nature or have human relationship because they no longer work. They satisfy their needs in direct actions on nature without transforming it. It is quite interesting to note that the masters' attitude is exactly similar to that of animals' because animals satisfy their need without modifying at all nature's structure. The masters' consciousness has finally become an arrested consciousness or one without any possibility of development.

However, the slave's consciousness has developed itself in the sense that, during the struggle, the slave has perceived and understood that for human life the natural world is far from constituting plenitude. But the true moment in the development of this consciousness intervenes in *labor*. Indeed, slaves are compelled to satisfy their masters' needs. In such a labor, they establish contact. From such a contact, in which slaves explore, study, manipulate, and transform objects, they acquire and build up science. Once again, for Hegel, labor—the confrontation between humans and nature, is an essential moment of human life because it truly marks the liberation of human beings from the so far terrifying clutches of nature.

Slaves—the laborers—are the true effective subjects; at the same time, because they transform nature and give it a human shape, they transform themselves, and reach levels of knowledge of things, and of themselves that are always superior. Human creative action in nature is at the same time the act of development and thought. Thus, human beings, by their will in labor accede to the only and true freedom. Slaves truly free themselves in labor. Therefore, struggle is at the heart of life or at the basis of all forms of development. Hegel writes: "Development, therefore, is not just a harmless and peaceful process of growth like that of organic life, but a hard and obstinate struggle with itself" (127).

Alienation and Objectification

By now, we understand that Hegel's constant problem is to restore totality while respecting particularities. It is a superior level of elaboration and a taking up of his initial problem: freedom can fully realize itself only within a society. For Hegel, the goal is the unity of the particular will with the universal will. All this can only happen in a state that recognizes each individual particularity and at the same time gives it a meaning.

It is also important to retain the fundamental Hegelian idea, according to which the economic regime forms a totality, an organic ensemble obeying objective and independent laws of desires or human will. For Hegel also, when individuals strive towards personal goals, the global result is different for each individual project. He says: "The labor of the individual for his own wants is just as much a satisfaction of those others as of himself, and the satisfaction of his own he attains only by the labor of others" (377).

Labor is what creates value. The elaboration of this concept provides Hegel with a solution to the problem of overcoming the opposition between subject and object. Labor thus defines a double relation: the one human beings keep with nature and the one they keep with each other in society. Therefore, for Hegel, labor is the starting point to study society and the development of freedom within. And the transcending of bestial needs is only possible with labor.

It is remarkable how, in his analysis of human objectification in labor, Hegel practically develops a historical materialist explanation of the social and cultural facts. In his *Philosophy of Right*, he writes:

> The multiplicity of objects and situations, which excite interest, is the stage on which theoretical education develops. This education consists in possessing not simply a multiplicity of ideas and facts, but also a flexibility and rapidity of mind, ability to pass from one idea to another, to grasp complex and general relations, and so on. It is the education of the understanding in every way, and so also the building up of language. Practical education acquired through working, consists first in the automatically recurrent need for something to do and the habit of simply being busy; next, in the strict adaptation of one's activity according not only to the nature of the material worked on, but also, and especially, to the pleasure of other workers; and family, in a habit, produced by this discipline, of objective activity and universally recognized aptitudes. (129).

Indeed, Hegel does not use proper Marxist concepts and terms but the essential point is that, through the Hegelian terminology, one can more or less detect the possibility of a transition to a Marxist explanation.

However, the Hegelian analysis of the labor concept as a means for the objectification of human essence is mostly interesting in the sense that it allows us to apprehend a certain evolution in the conceptualization of the problem of alienation. Alienation and objectification reveal themselves as indivisible in a common dialectic. And nature—the material foundation of human existence—is the scene of such an alienation-objectification-exteriorization. Thus, alienation appears as a necessity in which the dialectic of human accomplishment is possible. Indeed, there is a conceptual shift in the problematic of alienation: the understanding of alienation as the process of objectifying human beings in their labor products is no longer the same as in the previous understanding that we gave in *Marxist Theory*, in terms of politics and religion. At that time, alienation has meant a practice of estranging human being, which leads to their domination by alien powers such as God, Church, and political despots. Now, alienation is the necessary means to concretize human freedom.

This is how Hegel conceptualizes the problem between alienation and objectification: the objectification or exteriorization process, which identifies itself with the alienation process, is at the same time, if not essentially, the process by and through which human beings' freedom reaches effectiveness and concretely realizes itself in the world and in history. In short, alienation and liberation are somehow two perfectly identical terms of the same equation. During the 1968 riots in France, the avant-garde and autonomous Situationist group has made this understanding of Hegel very popular, in the form of a slogan: "Le chemin de la désalienation ne suit pas d'autre chemin que celui de l'alienation" [The suppression of alienation necessarily follows the same path as alienation].

Keeping the essential of this Hegelian analysis of human objectification/exteriorization, Marx simply radicalizes it. He retains, from Hegel, the fundamental idea that the objectification in labor is the historic engine driving the becoming world of human beings.

The Grandeur of the Hegelian Conception

In his *Manuscripts of 1844*, Marx reminds us of Hegel's depth in his conceptual elaboration of the objectification/alienation problematic. He declares:

> The outstanding achievement of Hegel's *Phänomenologie* and of its final outcome, the dialectic of negativity as the moving and generating principle, is thus first that Hegel conceives the self-creation of man as a process, conceives objectification as loss of the object, as alienation and as transcendence of this alienation; that he thus grasps the essence of *labor* and comprehends objective man—true, because real man—as the outcome of man's *own labor*. The *real, active* orientation of man to himself as a species-being, or his manifestation as a real species-being (i.e., as a human being), is only possible if he really brings out all his *species-powers*—something which in turn is only possible through the cooperative action of all of mankind, only as the result of history—and treats these powers as objects: and this, to begin with, is again only possible in the form of estrangement. (132)

For Marx, Hegel has the remarkable merit of conceiving human beings as endowed with a dynamic nature and not an immutable and static one. As we have shown in the master and slave dialectic, Masters are reduced to beings, meaning to "an empty abstraction," while slaves—the alienated workers—are the very expression of the creative process. They are the true creators of history for not only do they confront nature, which they work out, modify, transform, recreate, and reinvent, but also and at the same time, they transform themselves and self-generate.

Another aspect is that Hegel has justly perceived that the act of transforming nature and at the same time generating human beings themselves does not happen at the individual level but rather at the collective and social group level. The relations human beings maintain with nature are inseparable from the ones they maintain with themselves. Hegel thus has perfectly grasped the importance of negativity, both in its negative form (alienation) and in its positive one (negation of the negation), which is freedom. Negativity is thus both totality and the very principle of movement, development, or process.

Hegel has rightfully understood that the economic system inevitably generates a social inequality, which reveals itself in the existence of an extremely poor social group. He writes:

> When civil society is in a state of unimpeded activity, it is engaged in expanding internally in population and industry. The amassing of wealth is intensified by generalizing (a) the linkage of men by their needs, and (b) the methods of preparing and distributing the means to satisfy these needs, because it is from

this double process of generalization that the largest profits are derived. That is one side of the picture. The other side is the subdivision and restriction of particular jobs. This results in the dependence and distress of the class tied to work of that sort, and these again entail inability to feel and enjoy the broader freedoms and especially the intellectual benefits of civil society. (149)

Hegel perfectly understands that the development of mechanization and the ensuing division of social labor imply a total dehumanization of workers. He also perceives that the capitalist economic system, when it reaches a certain level of development, is led to colonial conquests in order to secure outlets and markets. He writes: "This inner dialectic of civil society thus drives it—or at any rate drives a specific civil society—to push beyond its own limits and seek markets, and so its necessary means of subsistence, in other lands which are either deficient in the goods it has over-produced, or else generally backward in industry, &c." (151).

Hegel analyzes the economic system with lucidity. For him, it is quite rational. This is explained by the fact that in his struggle against the residues of feudality, the economic system clearly appears to Hegel as a real and rational whole. The contradictions that he perceives in this system—the enriching of a class and the pauperization of the masses—cannot, for him, question the economic system, which is all historically founded in reality and reason. Hegel considers the social system a totality.

However, none of this prevents Marx from finding limitations in the Hegelian conception because, in some aspects, he finds it one-sided or not clear for itself.

Limits of the Hegelian Concept of Labor

According to Marx, Hegel confuses objectification—exteriorization of the human in nature and in the world—with alienation. This explains Hegel's insufficient social analysis, his inability to resolve the problems that he raises—at least to effectively resolve them—and turns his philosophical thought into a "mystification," which leads to a speculative idealism instead of a positive action. Therefore, Marx undertakes the critique of Hegel's "blunder," which consists in identifying objectification—the process by which human beings reify themselves, express and exteriorize themselves in nature through labor—with alienation, i.e., the process by which those objectified beings found themselves estranged, unable to recognize themselves. This "missed recognition" of oneself in the self-exteriorization is the foundation of human beings' miserable experience.

This painful experience reveals itself at the level of the relation between human beings and objects as well as at the level of inter-subjective relations in societies. Marx says: "An immediate consequence of the fact that man is estranged from the product of his labor, from his life activity, from his species-being, is the *estrangement of man* from *man*. When man confronts himself, he confronts the *other* man. What applies to another man's relation to his work, to the product of his labor and to himself, also holds of man's relation to the other man, and to the other man's labor and object of labor." (69)

According to Marx, objectification in itself is not alienation, nor does it coincide with a kind of existential unhappiness. On the contrary—as Hegel has perceived it—it is the only means to unite human beings with nature and to open the door to progress because human beings transform nature, shape the world, and stamp it with their creative power. However, why are objectified human beings still alienated, lost, and estranged from their labor? Why doesn't society appear as the very expression of their will instead of being a dominating and estranged will? This is where Hegel and Marx part company. For Hegel, alienation is a sort of existential category, inherent to human life, and which objectifies itself in labor. For Marx, the alienation of human beings in their objectification—in their productive activity—is a phenomenon that is linked to some determined historical forms in human society. More precisely, for Marx, "The *alienation* of the worker in his product means not only that his labor becomes an object, an *external* existence, but that it exists *outside him*, independently, as something alien to him, and that it becomes a power on its own confronting him" (63).

Does Hegel stop this dialectic of alienation at the very moment he connects it with objectification? In reality, this aspect of the problem that has triggered Marx's criticism is only a moment in this vast dialectic. Hegel did see that the objectification, which generates wealth and the social and economic life in general, also generates a new form of alienation. However, this time the concept of alienation is going to have another meaning, which is explained in what Hegel calls "Civil Society," which is precisely the result of the process of human beings' objectification. We can already say that, reprising the Hegelian critique of the new civil society, Marx will go into it and radicalize it.

In terms of fending off suffering, Freud describes the therapeutic effect of labor:

> When there is no special disposition in a person, which imperatively prescribes what direction his interests in life shall take, the ordinary professional work that is open to everyone can play the part assigned to it by Voltaire's wise advice. It is not possible, within the limits of a short survey, to discuss adequately the significance of work for the economics of the libido. No other technique for the conduct of life attaches the individual so firmly to reality as laying emphasis on work; for his work at least gives him a secure place in a portion of reality, in the human community. The possibility it offers of displacing a large amount of libidinal components, whether narcissistic, aggressive or even erotic, on to professional work and on to the human relations connected with it lends it a value by no mean second to what it enjoys as something indispensible to the preservation and justification of existence in society. Professional activity is a source of special satisfaction if it is a freely chosen one—if, that is to say, by means of sublimation, it makes possible the use of existing inclinations, of persisting or

constitutionally reinforced instinctual impulses. And yet as a path to happiness, work is not highly prized by men. They do not strive after it as they do after other possibilities of satisfaction. The great majority of people only work under the stress of necessity, and this natural aversion to work raises most difficult social problems. (27)

Marx echoes this Freudian position. For him, workers maintain a relation of pure exteriority with the objects that their own labor has produced. The object, which is materialized labor, becomes an autonomous and estranged reality facing workers. The alienating relations between workers and their own products are necessarily conditioned by another estrangement at the very level of the production activity or the externalizing activity. Therefore, labor is not workers' fulfillment nor is it a free and creative activity, which makes them feel that they are truly human. Marx explains it clearly:

> First, the fact that labor is *external* to the worker, i.e., it does not belong to his intrinsic nature; that in his work, therefore, he does not affirm himself but denies himself, does not feel content but unhappy, does not develop freely his physical and mental energy but mortifies his body and ruins his mind. The worker therefore only feels himself outside his work, and in his work feels outside himself. He feels at home when he is not working, and when he is working he does not feel at home. His labor is therefore not voluntary, but coerced; it is *forced labor*. It is therefore not the satisfaction of a need; it is merely a *means* to satisfy needs external to it. Its alien character emerges clearly in the fact that as soon as no physical or other compulsion exists, labor is shunned like the plague. External labor, labor in which man alienates himself, is a labor of self-sacrifice, of mortification. Lastly, the external character of labor for the worker appears in the fact that it is not his own, but someone else's, that it does not belong to him, that in it he belongs, not to himself, but to another. Just as in religion the spontaneous activity of the human imagination, of the human brain and the human heart, operates on the individual independently of him—that is, operates as an alien, divine or diabolical activity—so is the worker's activity not his spontaneous activity. It belongs to another; it is the loss of his self.
>
> As a result, therefore, man (the worker) only feels himself freely active in his animal functions—eating, drinking, procreating, or at most in his dwelling and in dressing-up, etc.; and in his human functions he no longer feels himself to be anything but an animal. What is animal becomes human and what is human becomes animal.
>
> Certainly eating, drinking, procreating, etc., are also genuinely human functions. But taken abstractly, separated from the sphere of all other human activity and turned into sole and ultimate ends, they are animal functions. (65-66).

Thus workers do not happily and enthusiastically work to realize themselves. They simply work because they are compelled to do so to guarantee their survival. Such labor is mandatory, and in the end, it is forced labor. Marx says: "it is therefore not the satisfaction of a need; it is merely a *means* to satisfy needs external to it" (66). Thus, labor, is synonymous with self-sacrifice, mortification, and total ruin. At another level, labor is exteriority in the sense that workers' labor does not properly belong to them but to others: workers are not their own masters but slaves of others. Thus, Marx explains that workers feel free only in the acts of eating, drinking, procreating, etc., which are ultimately animal.

In this sense, Fanon, the theorist of decolonization takes issue with the problems that Hegel's master-slave dialectic encounters in its translation into a post-colonial context. In the passage below from *Black Skin White Masks* (1967), Fanon, of Marxist background himself, revises the dialectic to suggest that it underestimates the White master's dominance over Black slaves in Africa and Europe:

> I hope I have shown that here the master differs basically from the master described by Hegel. For Hegel, there is reciprocity; here the master laughs at the consciousness of the slave. What he wants from the slave is not recognition but work. In the same way, the slave here is in no way identifiable with the slave who loses himself in the object and finds in his work the source of his liberation. The Negro wants to be like the master. Therefore, he is less independent than the Hegelian slave. In Hegel, the slave turns away from the master and turns toward the object. Here, the slave turns toward the master and abandons the object. (220-21)

Thus, there is a great difference between the meaning of the term labor for Fanon and Hegel. For Fanon (1973), "Absolute praxis is represented by violence and the militant is the man who works" (85), thus identifying labor with violence. There is already an opposition in the use of the term labor between Hegel and Marx as we have shown. Most likely, Fanon and Marx refer to labor as in political economy, the concrete labor that the worker provides, and which can be measured in terms of time and money par opposition to Hegel's notion of abstract labor we have just explained. For him, the only real labor is the labor of the spirit; any other form of labor is common to all surviving animals.

We are not going any further with this alienation/objectification debate as it leads to issues of Adam Smith's influence, money, exchange, and private property, and more importantly to the notion of a division of labor division. Suffice it to say that are they are parts or moments of the vast Hegelian dialectic. Hegel has seen that the objectification, which generates wealth and the social and economic life in general, also generates a new form of alienation in the civil society in the form of the state, hierarchy, merchandise, and money.

Thus, I am closing the chapter with the help of the Université de Paris Professor Henri Denis's *L' "Economie" de Marx: histoire d'un échec* [*Marx's "Economy": The Story of a Failure*] (1992). This book provides a sharp criticism of Marx's economic theory in favor of a Hegelian approach. It seems that at some point in his theorizing of the capitalist "economy," agent Marx has deviated from the path of the Hegelian dialectic and become intoxicated by Ricardo and Smith.

For Denis—who has made sure to remind us that despite his unfinished work, Marx has essentially fulfilled the task that he has assigned himself—most of Marx's economic theories do not correspond to reality. Marx has used two irreconcilable sources: Ricardo's theory of value and the Hegelian dialectic. Eventually, he opted for Ricardo and abandoned the conception of capital that he has developed under the influence of Hegelian thought.

Hegel does not consider the loss of "ethical life" or alienation an absolute ill that must be suppressed by returning to community life. For Hegel, merchant society is a "cunning of reason," which allows people to get close to freedom in a movement that first seems to estrange them from it. On the other hand, Marx demands the immediate happening of an absolute and rational rule. As in the case of other "rationalists," Denis thinks that it goes together with a materialist conception of reality that is as removed as possible from Hegelian idealism.

He recommends the following: "As far as we are concerned, it is already neatly appearing . . . that certain theses that Marx has developed in 1857 and 1858—and abandoned later—should be resumed in order to formulate a theory of value that would be a pure application of the Hegelian logic. It would be a starting point for a dialectic analysis of the capitalist economy" (200).

Hegel and Haiti

In the work of Hegel and Marx, alienation is the dialectic of alienation. They understand that history goes toward an increasingly total affirmation of humankind. Now here is a vital point in dialectic: that affirmation, even if posited as history's ultimate end, is not, for all that, considered a primary given. Freedom is never a starting point but always a result of a long process. Hegel says: "Of the Absolute it must be said it is essentially a result, that only in the end is it what it truly is" (81-82).

The history of individuals is only a reproduction of the history of nations, which in turn is the reproduction of universal history. Hegel and Marx's problem, thus, is to understand humans' life as it manifests itself throughout history, in its total aspects. They conceive humanity's history as a problem of alienation: the history of humans is the history of their alienation.

Yes, Hegel understands that the alienation tearing up human life is perfectly rational. It finds its justification and legitimacy in the very logic of the historical process. However, all this seems to go over Buck-Morss's head. She has not realized that Hegel is still judging our epoch.

In her *Hegel, Haiti, and Universal Story,* Buck-Morss becomes frustrated because, for her, Hegel has not pursued further his thought on the "great experiment" that is Haiti's Revolution. She states: "What is clear is that in an effort to become more erudite in African studies during the 1820s, Hegel was in fact becoming dumber" (73). One has to wonder what postmodernist scholar has the arrogance to address the Master philosopher of Berlin in such a way. Not that Hegel is out of critical range, on the contrary! We understand that postmodernist scholars have acquired the right to criticize the existing organizations of culture. It also seems that the task of expressing revolutionary positions is left to them and it often leads to expressing them in detail with ill-conceived charges, as in the case of Buck-Morss. This type of spectacular postmodernist show off criticism is just mystification. She says: "He [Hegel] repeated his lectures on philosophy of history every two years from 1822 to 1830s, adding empirical material from his reading of the European experts on world history. It is sadly ironic that the more faithful his lectures reflected Europe's conventional scholarly wisdom on African society, the less enlightened and more bigoted they became" (73-74). Her conclusion in this matter is that Hegel has distorted his theory in order to fit his philosophy of history. That is really misjudging Hegel. The English philosopher Walter T. Stace (1954) reminds us:

> The philosophy of Hegel is not something simple invented of nothing by himself and flung at random into an astonished world. It is not the pet theory of some erratic genius, nor is it merely one theory among many rivals. The true author of it is, not so much Hegel, as the toiling and thinking human spirit, the universal spirit of humanity getting itself uttered through this individual. It is the work of ages. It has its roots deep in the past. It is the accumulated wisdom of the years, the last phase of the one "universal philosophy. For the truth is, to use a phrase of Hegel's, neither new nor old, but permanent. Yet Hegel, too, is profoundly original. It recognizes all past truth, absorbs it into itself and advances. (lx)

Hegel is a consequent and anti-capitalist revolutionary and Marx is his revelation. Maybe that is what is missing: Buck-Morss needs to look at Hegel with Marxian lenses and looks at Marx with Hegelian lenses. Indeed, the pursuit of the criticism of Hegel's thought is one and the same as the criticism of Marx's thought. It would then be clearer that Hegel and Marx formulate the exigency of transcending a world where humankind can no longer recognize itself nor feel at home. That goal has never left them.

The literature abounds with testimonies about Hegel's sharpness. Hyppolite states: "Hegel does not construct the world with pseudo-concepts of the academy; he takes seriously "the pain, the work, and the patience of the negative." His concept is not the rational in the ordinary sense of the term, but the enlargement of thought, of reason which turns out to be capable of sublating itself as mere thought, as mere understanding, and to be capable of continuing to think itself in the beyond of mere abstract thought" (103).

Buck-Morss reluctantly recognizes Tavares as the one who has first started to explore, deepen, and explain the topic of San Domingo Revolution and the Birth of Haiti as a double event and the historic sources—not just one—of the famous "figure of consciousness," better known in the *Phenomenology* as a "Lordship and Bondage" dialectic: it is part of his 1990 Ph. D thesis, which he continues to supplement with more precision in articles and presentations on the subject. Moreover, Tavares is no more a victim of Euro-American academic hegemony than Buck-Morss, who seems to be unaware of that. Tavares's advantage is that he is not a postmodernist.

In his film *Haiti: The End of the Chimères* (2004), Charles Najman interviews the Haitian writer Gary Victor, who explains that Haitians are victims of a big myth, which makes them believe that the 1804 Revolution saw a victory for slaves freeing themselves: "In fact, 1804 was a victory for the owner class. Affranchised slaves allied themselves to the old generals, who were officers in the French Army. So, the majority of Black slaves ended up in the same situation, if not worse: in a state of apartheid where political and economic power belonged to former owners, mostly mulattos and a few Blacks." Thus, Haitians are still slaves. The Black masses' whole history has been a quest for freedom. Now, they have finally realized that they have been robbed of power, a country, and a state. Thus, Haitians are still slaves just like the other modern slaves peopling this planet.

In terms of the Haitian Revolution—so dear to Buck-Morss—we say that Haiti's present problems were already contained in the 1804 Revolution. There are victories that are defeats and there are defeats that are victories. Haiti may have been great for accomplishing the human rights revolution on its soil but its revolution is not just incomplete; it has failed: it is a bourgeois revolution. Its victory is the victory of the owner class as we can see it today.

The history of the intellectual and political leaders who control, produce, and diffuse culture in Haiti is the history of their submission to all powers. They limit themselves to exalting their alienation or elaborating it artistically and intellectually, without questioning their neo-colonial situation or fighting against the totality of those alienations. Has Hegel seen the Haitian Revolution for what it is? We will know some day.

Otherwise, the dominant Haitian intelligentsia and the dominant racial culture they diffuse are easily understood when one recognizes their class situation. The nationalists (Blacks) or the liberals (mulattos) use the color card at the expense of the poor. As we have already explained, the intelligentsia, its ideas and dominant culture, are the intelligentsia, the ideas, and culture of the dominant class. But here in Haiti or in South Africa the struggle of the dominant class to stay dominant is lived under the cover of color.

Buck-Morss cannot just criticize the side of Hegel's "Theory of History" by ignoring or falsely criticizing the "Theory of Society" side. We do want to know the new limits in Hegel's thought, to know in what way Haiti or our time have become more profoundly what they were in Hegel's and Marx's days. An unreal world has inspired them and that world has not become any more real since then. The world has barely changed since Hegel and Marx: the dominant ideas are still the ruling class's ideas. Above all, today's dominant ideas are the same as the ones that used to rule in Hegel's and Marx's days, which is not surprising because today's ruling class is the same as the one that used to rule in Hegel's and Marx's days. On the other hand, something has changed: these very dominant ideas rule much more today than in Hegel's and Marx's days.

Buck-Morss issues another of her ill-conceived postmodernist-style charges:

> We are left with only two alternatives. Either Hegel was the blindest of all the blind philosophers of freedom in Enlightenment Europe, surpassing Locke and Rousseau by far in his ability to block out reality right in front of his nose (the *print* right in front of his nose at the breakfast table); or Hegel knew—knew about real slaves revolting successfully against real masters, and he elaborated his dialectic of lordship and bondage deliberately within this contemporary context. (50)

Kostas Papaioannou (2001) explains how Hegel, sensing upcoming criticisms, has made sure to indicate what is a true refutation of a philosophical system: to really refute a philosophy, one must a priori recognize the essentiality and necessity of its stand-point. In Hegel's terms: "With respect to the refutation of a philosophical system, . . . the refutation must not come from outside, that is, it must not proceed from assumptions lying outside the system in question and inconsistent with it. The system need only refuse to recognize those assumptions; the *defect* is a defect only for him who starts from the requirements and demands based on those assumptions" (580-81).

If one does not recognize the premises of Hegel's thought and does not feel the need that they translate nor the exigencies they carry, such refutation remains profoundly alien, resolutely external to its subjects. Thus, for any critic who does not presuppose as an established fact the negation of alienation, the total freedom of the self-conscious subject, and the radical transformation of society, there cannot be any real criticism of Hegel's theory or Marx's for that matter. For "the genuine refutation must penetrate the opponent's stronghold and meet him on his own ground; no advantage is gained by attacking him somewhere else and defeating him where he is not. The only possible refutation must therefore consist, in the first place, in recognizing its standpoint as essential and necessary and then going on to raise that standpoint to the higher one through its own immanent dialect" (581).

Postmodernist scholars cannot criticize part of this world while accepting all the rest of the world. To criticize Hegel's thought—and Marx's for that matter—it is not enough to know their theories: one must be able to criticize the world that contains them. It is only by criticizing this world that one can criticize the theories of this world. Lacing one's theory with "race" and "racism" or sprinkling it with "Black" and "Blackness" changes nothing.

One of Hegel's merits is to have given a perfectly criticizable form to the theory of religion and the state and Marx's is to do the same with economy, to drive it into a corner, and to give it a perfectly unacceptable form. In the same way, in Marx and Ludwig Feuerbach's days—and thanks to Hegel—the criticism of religion and the state has consisted in the criticism of Hegel's thought; today—and thanks to Marx—the criticism of economy consists in the criticism of Marx's thought: it is the prerequisite to any criticism. To the chagrin of all the reviewers who have emphatically hailed Buck-Morss for her "overdue" criticism of Hegel, we have this to say: after their respective deaths, 127 and 179 years ago, Marx and Hegel are still avant-garde. What was open to criticism in their theories has still not been criticized and what was revolutionary in their theories is still revolutionary because it has never been verified anywhere.

In terms of the "end of history" issue, see August von Cieszkowski's *Prolegomena zur Historiosophie* (1838) [*Prolégomènes à l'historiosophie*], in which he focuses on Hegel's view of world history and reforms it to better accommodate Hegelian Philosophy itself by dividing it into past, present, and future. He argues that we have gone from Art (the Past), which was a stage of contemplating the Real, to Philosophy (the Present), which is a contemplation of the Ideal, and that since Hegel's philosophy was the summing-up and perfection of Philosophy, the time of Philosophy was up, and the time for a new era has dawned—the era of Action.

Nowhere in Hegel's work is the future mentioned. Therefore, he sets out to apply the dialectic to the philosophy of history and thus to reveal the future. Philosophy can draw the laws of history only as far as the past is concerned. However, for Cieszkowski, either the laws of dialectic are universal and unavoidable—if so, they should show their reality in history—or they are precarious, partial, and insufficient. In such a case, they cannot reveal themselves in the other domains of knowledge. For him, history is an organic totality and the future is a part of it, just like the past and the present.

Therefore, Cieszkowski's criticism of Hegel takes care of the valid objection against Hegel's philosophy: are we at the end of History? For him, not only does the future remain open, but also it is also possible to know it. Of course, such knowledge cannot be about particular contents, but must be about the essence of the future, of progress, that is if dialectic is true.

Hegel and Marx have done nothing but use the available theories of their times. They know how to make use of them and we approve what they have done with them. We consider them worthy of criticism and above any denigration or insult.

Chapter Six

Labor in Traditional Africa

In his effort to explain Africans in relation to labor and time, the Economics Professor Emmanuel Kamdem provides us with some fundamental characteristics of labor in traditional Africa in his "Temps et travail en Afrique" [Time and Labor in Africa] (2007). Relying mostly on the Zairian philosopher P. E. A. Elungu (1987), Kamdem detects a rupture between the world of labor and the social milieu around it which is created by the imposition of capitalist techniques of production. He succeeds in reaching his goal of finding what prevents African workers from being completely molded into the enterprise system. His goal is, of course, to find how to better insert the African worker into the capitalist industrial system that has invaded Africa.

Kamdem does mention Marx—but not Hegel—yet, from what I see, his article is the synthesis of Hegel's and Marx's understanding of alienation. For me, he shows that Africa has always been Hegelian. Had the master philosopher of Berlin come across such material, there would be no doubt as to where the Spirit would emerge. Kamdem explains how alienated labor in a capitalist society is just as Marx says. He also explains how Africans' high level of sociability has been estranged to the profit of lucrative labor. Thus, Hegel is right: human beings are estranged from themselves. They are no longer total.

For Kamdem, labor as a means of production and transformation of nature carries constraints and is often one of the main sources of human alienation. Quoting Elungu, Kamdem writes: "La société urbaine, comme la société étatique, plus englobante, est une société constituée et fondée par le travail; le pouvoir lui-même se subordonne en quelque sorte à ces exigences du travail et lui sert très souvent d'instrument" [Urban societies, like the more inclusive state society, is founded and consists of labor. In some ways, power itself is subordinated to the exigencies of labor and often plays the role of instrument] (234). Kamdem sees an aristocratic conception of life, which led to a split between labor activities—reserved for slaves—and other forms of social or recreational activities. Such a conception of life, torn between labor for some (slaves) and permanent distraction for others (ruling class), is very different from what can be observed in traditional African societies. In such societies, labor activity differs very little from other dominant social activities in which human beings are not detached from social relations and symbols. Hegel and Marx have perceived that in the Roman world, those who work are different from those who devote their time to leisure activities. In traditional Africa, the working individual is also the one communicating, singing and dancing.

In traditional Africa, labor is as Hegel explains it. Labor appears as a true source of self-affirmation and self-liberation. It allows human beings to acquire a social status; the rest of their activities, particularly life outside labor, are going to be determined and organized according of the prime and priority activity that is labor.

Labor as a Factor of Life Preservation and Prolongation

The organization and functioning of traditional African societies rest on a fundamental principle: the permanence of life. Thus, it appears to be a society that is essentially "covital" as Elungu would say. The protection and prolongation of life constitute the finality of all existence. The entire traditional African culture is founded on this primary fact. On a practical level, the idea of permanent life is at the heart of one of the most lively and religious traditions in traditional as well as in modern African society: it is the cult of the ancestors. The determinant foundation of African religions is: "the dead are not dead, they live in the blowing and moving wind." In other words, death is not an end in itself; it is only a transition between the visible and the invisible world. For traditional Africans, to die does not mean to definitely disappear for good but rather, they take on an eternal new life. Human beings who pass away return to the eternal source of permanent existence. That is the time to rejoice." Such is Africans' attitude in front of death, which is far from being seen as a victory over life, but rather, the beginning of a new one.

That is how one can understand the representation that traditional Africans have of labor. Because life is permanent and must be lived up, nothing, and absolutely nothing must make it painful or shorten it. All the activities human beings undertake should fall within the scope of prolonging life. Kamden quotes Elungu: "La vie économique ne s'impose pas à la vie; le travail, loin de constituer le principe de différenciation entre les hommes par la distribution des tâches et des rôles sociaux, suit, au contraire, un clivage que la vie en s'instaurant, en se différenciant, établit parmi les homes, c'est à dire, la différence des sexes" [Economic life does not impose itself onto life; labor, far from being the principle of differentiation among human beings by assigning social tasks and roles, instead follows a cleavage, which life—introducing itself, differentiating itself—establishes among human beings, i.e., sexual differences] (72).

Moreover, labor should in no way constitute a means of domination within societies, let alone a source of enslavement and depersonalization of individuals. It means that life or the existence of human beings does not have to suffer from the exercise of any labor activity, in the sense that it is a source of various physical, moral, and temporal constraints. Kamden quotes Elungu: "Jamais au sein de la communauté clanique, le travail ne donne l'occasion à l'homme de s'aliéner l'autre homme parce que jamais il n'est considéré comme une marchandise que l'on peut s'approprier par toutes sortes de moyens. Le travail n'est pas encore alienable, n'est encore ni l'occasion ni la source d'aliénation pour les autres" [Never within the clanic community has labor given human beings the opportunity to estrange themselves from other human beings, because they are never considered commodities that one can appropriate by all sorts of means. Labor is not yet alienable and is neither an opportunity nor the source of alienation for others] (73).

For traditional Africans, labor is life, not because they spend all their lives working to live, but because labor and life are tightly woven. The organization of one should not have a negative influence on the functioning of the other. Both find themselves in a harmonious and cohesive situation and are not opposed or split, as is the case in industrialized countries.

At another level, labor is perceived not only as a production activity but also, and above all, as an activity of distraction and leisure. Therefore, it is inconceivable that one can accomplish any task without chatting with a neighbor or colleague from time to time, or distracting oneself by singing or having a quick dance. From a Taylorian approach to labor, which is predominant in the Western world, such parallel activities are translated into "useless" gestures or movements that considerably perturb the individual in a work process and reduce the "productive" labor time, thus compromising its effective realization.

For Africans, such distracting and recreational activities during labor are absolutely necessary because they allow them to live the labor process in total harmony with their social life of games, words, feasts, and leisure. Therefore, to reproach Africans for introducing such activities into the formal framework of labor is the equivalent of depriving them of fundamental rights to survive, work, enjoy themselves, and live at the same time. One can now understand why African workers have a paradoxical and negative perception of industrial labor, the lucrative one imported from the Western world.

First, industrial and lucrative labor, because of the way it is organized and the conditions of it process, compels individuals to evolve in a very impoverished and traumatizing environment of interpersonal relations, while social life mostly rests on the warmth and spontaneity of such relations. Indeed, from birth African children find themselves in a social milieu which is essentially characterized by the density, richness, and diversity of human relations. They live "in a universe of total gratification" in which they are constantly surrounded, solicited, and adulated by the ensemble of the family group members (father, mother, aunt, uncle, grandparents etc.), which contributes to develop a very happy social ambiance around them.

Second, industrial and lucrative labor is a permanent source of various constraints, which contribute mostly to the dehumanization of the African individual. African workers do not often find in it that affective and rational dimension that just mentioned as one of the fundamental characteristics of their social lives. In Africa, familiar expressions such as "White man's labor never ends" or "This is a White man's labor," illustrate this reality: industrial and lucrative labor holds sway over individuals so strongly that they develop the feeling of not having the necessary time to live. Far from being part of the normal and natural life, such a labor rather contributes to compromise and dangerously perturbs it.

Labor as a Community Activity

Another determinant factor characterizes labor in traditional African societies: the total dependence of individuals in relation to groups. Individuals' lives and labors are founded on those of the groups in which they belong. Any attempt at detachment from the group or any expression of behavior that is opposed to the group appears as a violation of one of the fundamental principles of social organization and regulation. Kamdem cites Elungu: "La société, la culture comme expression de cette vision fondamentale du monde ne sera ni fondée sur les vertus individuelles et justifiée par elles, ni non plus fondée sur un groupe d'individus et expliquée par eux" [Society and culture, as expressions of this fundamental vision of the world, will neither be based on individual virtues that justify it, nor will it be founded on a group of individuals that explain it] (76).

In traditional economies, mostly of subsistence, labor activities (cultivation and hunting and gathering) are organized in the form of community labors during which each individual is assigned a precise role to play. In industrial development economies, such community vision of labor is going to translate into a systematic refusal of a fragmented and individualized labor. Here, one can well judge African workers' profound misery in an industrial setting. They are prisoners of fixed labor position that they must occupy for a determined amount of time while being deprived of human warmth, which the spontaneous conversation with colleagues provides. No doubt, to some extent, the Western worker also experiences such a misery.

The organization of labor as a community activity mostly aims at erasing individual differences, maintaining a system of effort sharing and compensation among individuals, taking into account the capacity to produce. Such a system offers a safety valve, which allows the attenuation of certain inequalities in labor, in terms of productivity and retribution. It is not based on individual performances as a privileged criterion of workers' evaluation.

The Sphere of Economic Activities in Africa

African scholars themselves or Western Africanists have conducted in-depth economic research among all kinds of nations, societies, communities, ethnic groups, and clans in Africa. By comparing and combining the various findings, it becomes easy to see the central axis, the common elements that are particular to diverse Negro African economic systems as well as their regime of appropriation and repartitioning of products.

In Africa, as well as elsewhere, the land is the most important condition in people's material lives. Because of a subsistence economy, life in Africa depends even more brutally on the land. At times, the land becomes a cult object as in the case of the Gikuyu myth that Jomo Kenyatta (1953) cites: "The earth is the 'mother' of the tribe for the reason that the mother bears her burden for about eight or nine moons while the child is in her womb, and then for a short period of suckling. But it is the soil that feeds the child through a lifetime; and after death it is the soil that nurses the spirits of the dead for eternity. Thus the earth is the most sacred thing above all that dwells in or on it" (21). In Negro African traditions, the land has always belonged to the first occupant and has always been a collective appropriation.

Instruments of production also constitute one of the platforms for Negro African cultural specificities. According to Claude Meillassoux (1964), the exclusive usage of tools in Africa is quite striking: "One . . . characteristic of traditional economies is the use of quasi-direct techniques of productions: the product of labor is obtained almost directly. In other words, the producer interposes only instruments, which have been made with few prior operations between himself and the object of his labor" (90).

Tools could go from a knife to a mortar and pestle, a saber, a spear, a bow and arrow to a canoe, a trap, an anvil or a net among many others. In relation to the machine, Marx says:

> All fully developed machinery consists of three essentially different parts, the motor mechanism, the transmitting mechanism, and finally the tool or working machine. The motor mechanism is that which puts the whole in motion. It either generates its own motive power, life the steam-engine, the caloric engine, the electromagnetic machine, &c., or it receives its impulse from some already existing natural force, like the water-wheel from a head of water, the wind-mill from wind, &c., the transmitting mechanism, composed of fly-wheels, shafting, toothed varied kinds, regulates the motion, changes its form where necessary, as fro instance, from linear to circular, and divides and distributes it among the working machines. These two first parts of the whole mechanism are there, solely for putting the working machines in motion by means of which motion the subject of labor is seized upon and modified as desired. (352-53)

Thus, next to the machine, simplicity characterizes the tool. Here, the criterion of differentiation between machines—simple or complex—and tools is the human presence. Both machines and tools carry out a human program, thus implementing human labor. In the production process, human beings, the laborers, are at the center and they can be free people that own the instruments of production or slaves.

In Africa, slaves have had a very particular status. We begin with Meillassoux's study of slavery among the Gouro people of Ivory Coast. Although it is a general study, one finds the essential points common to most African societies:

> Particularly in the savannah, slavery reached high proportions only lately. The Gouro traditionally practiced a form of domestic slavery, which applied to no more than a handful of persons. The number was small: a village of 300 people would count less than twenty slaves. Domestic slaves were subject to the command of their masters or their wives and were used for fieldwork, carrying water, building huts, etc. The most skillful and those who enjoyed the confidence of their masters undertook more important tasks, such as weaving, fishing, or hunting the elephant on their behalf. Even though they were entirely subject to the authority of the master, who has the power of life and death over them and could sell them, domestic slaves were associated with the kinship system: they shared the communal meal, eating it with their masters; they might even inherit from them if they have no heirs. They were married according to the exogamous rules of the lineage to women of other lineages, usually to other slaves for whom a bride-price was paid; but sometimes a higher bride-price was paid to marry one to a free woman. The doyen of the community adopted the children of slaves and, with the passing of the generations, the distinction of rank became blurred to vanishing point. (203-4)

He adds:

> Avec les guerres de Samory (1830-1900) s'accrut le nombre d'esclaves-marchandises échangés désormais contre des vivres et des fusils. L'accroissement du nombre d'esclaves ne s'accompagna pas d'une réorganization de l'économie gouro susceptible de les intégrer efficacement comme producteurs. La cellule communautaire était organiquement limitée en extension. Au-delà de ceux qu'elle pouvait incorporer, les hommes riches acquirent des esclaves pour étendre leur autorité sur un plus vaste groupe, mais sans avoir les moyens de contrainte ou de police nécessaires pour les mettre efficacement au travail. A l'exception donc des esclaves domestiques, les autres tendaient à jouer pour leur maître le rôle de biens de prestige dont l'efficacité économique était, elle aussi, douteuse. [With Samory Touré's wars, the number of slave-commodities increased and henceforth exchanged against food and rifles. However, this increase was not accompanied by a reorganization of a Gouro economy that would be likely to efficiently integrate them as producers. The community cell was organically limited in extension. Beyond those it could incorporate, rich men acquired slaves to extend their authority on a vaster group, but without having the means of constraint or the necessary police to ef-

ficiently put them to work. Thus, with the exception of domestic slaves, the others tended to play for their masters the role of goods of prestige whose economic efficiency was also doubtful]. (204)

One needs to add that in Africa, Slaves used to always work parallel to their masters in the production unit. The product then is the crystallization of both the masters' and slaves' labor and not the crystallization of the sole labor force. In other words, it is not the crystallization of an exclusive slaves' or workers' labor, which defines a social and economic system such as slave society, feudalism, and capitalism. In *Civilization or Barbarism* (1991), Diop explains that in this case, the position of slaves is not identical to the one found among the Athenian Thetes, the Spartan inferior Helots, or the Roman plebeians. He finds a common denominator in economies of the Asiatic type, Black Africa, China, India, Iran, and pre-Columbian America, etc.: an absence of slavery in the full sense of the term, as a mean of production, while "The Greek State was founded from birth on slavery and the intangibility of private land ownership"(225). If anything, the status of slaves in America can be compared to the ones in the stateless Libyan communities, the Ageans, Asians, Philistines, Etruscans, or Sicules. Diop explains: "The point is that in traditional Negro Africa, servile labor has never been the basis of the social and economic life, even in the case of the most despotic ones such as the Medieval Sudanese Kingdoms or the sixteen century Kingdom of Kongo, as Coquery-Vidrovitch explains: "the authority of the sovereign never replaced the patriarchal organization. At most, it involved a superimposed bureaucracy, which respected the structures of rural life" (135).

The System of Propriety

In the traditional economic organization, the tools, instruments of production and slaves have never been the exclusive possession or private propriety of an individual in the Western sense. Masters really do exist and they are embodied in the personality of the *paterfamilias*, the eldest or doyen, or the most senior member of the community. However, tools as well as labor product remain the collective propriety of the whole unit of production. As Kenyatta explains in terms of land organization among the Gikuyu of Kenya:

> After the death of the father, the land passed on to his sons, the eldest son took his father's place. At this juncture, the system of land tenure changed a little, there was no one who could regard the land as "mine," all would call it 'our land." The eldest son who has assumed the title of *moramati* (titular or trustee) has no more rights than his brothers except the title; he could not sell the land without the agreement of his brothers who had the same full cultivation rights on the pieces of land, which they cultivated as well as those which were cultivated by their respective mothers. (32)

While in traditional Africa we find loose and flexible principles of property owning, in Greece, Diop finds a very sharp and advanced notion of private propriety. He says:

> One of the fundamental traits of the city institution is the extraordinary care with which the Eupatridae victors protect the private property of lands to a point of divinizing it. The divinization of private property is specifically Indo-European: it is common to Greece, Rome, and Aryan India. The individualization of nomadic life reveals itself in all the aspects of Indo-European private legislation; two contiguous houses cannot have a common wall: a small and neutral space must separate them; the party wall is a sacrilege or a crime *strictu sensu*. Even in the beyond, families must remain rigorously separate. (132-33)

For Kenyatta, in Africa "the system of land tenure was never tribal tenure, nor was there any customary law, which gave any particular chief or group of chiefs any power over lands other than the lands of their own family groups" (32). It is the same thing when it comes to the circulation of products. Meillassoux says:

> [The harvest] is stored in community granaries under the direct or indirect control of the elder. The second brother or first wife is often the manager. The primary use for the produce is the feeding of the community, sometimes a temporary guest, a few relatives from a neighboring village, or the members of a *bo*. Usually, only a small portion is sold or exchanged. The doyen of the community is the axis around which the circulation of the goods revolves. The produce of the group goes to him, and then most if not all of it is returned to the members of the community. (32)

Thus in African societies, (1) the land, tools, and slaves are the collective propriety of the whole community of production, which itself is tied to the notion of the very "extended family"; (2) masters are the keepers of the community reserves; (3) the institution of slavery has never been in concert with a reorganization of the economy or a questioning of the old social organization. Production has never been based on the exclusive labor of slaves. The latter is often integrated into the parenthood relations, which unite the members of the productive unit. Under the strict supervision of the different members of the productive units, they organize the distribution, which is egalitarian because it obeys the exigencies of the same concept of parenthood.

Human Beings, Nature, and Society

As we have shown earlier, African culture does have its own particularities. Now, do we also have to deal with them from a particular angle? Does the phenomenon reflect the ontology, as Martin Heidegger would say? In short, do Negro Africans—from the very stuff they are made of—distinguish themselves from the Western type? We think that such a thesis is not plausible at all, except for the very few minds that are desperately trying to salvage metaphysics and turn their backs to objective and scientific data.

Science can rely on postulates. A postulate and all the constructions that come from it is true if it has a practical application and reveals itself useful to human praxis, without falling into some kind of utilitarianism. Moreover, no one needs to demonstrate any longer the universality of physics, cytology, anatomy, organic chemistry and their applications by medical technology. However, they do offer irrefutable proofs of (1) the biologic identity of humankind no matter what skin color or environment and (2) the telluric foundations of humans. To conclude with Marx:

> The life of species, both in [human] and animals consists physically in the fact that man (like the animal) lives on inorganic nature; and the more universal man (or the animal) is, the more universal is the sphere of inorganic nature on which he lives. Just as plants, animals, stones, air, light, etc., constitute theoretically a part of human consciousness, partly as object of natural science, partly as object of art—his spiritual inorganic nature, spiritual nourishment which he must first prepare to make palatable and digestible—so also in the realm of practice they constitute a part of human life and human activity. Physically man lives only on these products of nature, whether they appear in the form of food, heating, clothes, a dwelling, etc. The universality of man appears in practice precisely in the universality which makes all nature his *inorganic* body—both in as much as nature is (1) his direct means of life, and (2) the material, the object, and the instrument of his [her] life activity. Nature is man's *inorganic body*—nature that is insofar as it is not itself human body, with which he must remain in continuous interchange if he is not to die. That man's physical and spiritual life is linked to nature means simply that nature is linked to itself, for man is part of nature. (67)

Negro Africans experience needs in housing, warmth, food and others, and therefore they need to create the necessary objects for their lives. These "labor objects" can be found in nature such as certain fruits, leaves, and tree roots that sometimes need prior transformation. In any case, Negro Africans expend their own energy or labor force to assure their own existence. To compensate for their morphological insufficiencies, they create tools, which are commonly understood as artificial extensions for the purpose of reinforcing human natural organs: arrows and spears to hunt games, axes and hoes to dig, knock down trees, clear the way etc. To all these, one can add Negro African intellectual resources, imagination, efforts of reflection, and method.

Africans have never devoted themselves to these activities in isolation i.e., outside of a group of people or a society. In the equatorial forests as well as in the Sahelian or desert zones, Africans were never born outside a family structure and they have never produced outside an environment with collective norms of exchange. They have always lived in human groups, in societies that have their own structures and social needs, and in institutions of all kinds that oppose or identify themselves with particular individual's needs. In the process of production, exchange, and distribution of material goods, Africans have always maintained relationships with their fellow humans. Inside the productive family unit—most often united by a system of kinship—economic relations are egalitarian relations of cooperation and mutual aid.

Now, these relations can become exploitative between the whole productive community, holders of the means of existence, and slavery. Such relations also exist between the "free peasantry"—structured into castes—and the slaves on the one hand, and the feudal aristocracy on the other: the aristocracy and the "free peasantry systematically appropriate the slaves' labor and persona. The aristocracy partially appropriates the "free" citizens' labor fruit in corvée, taxes, or land rental charges.

Next to these material phenomena, there exist non-material ones or spiritual phenomena: Negro Africans experience desires, feelings, passion, joy, and enthusiasm, and they do have an "inner world." They are endowed with thought, reason, consciousness; they conceive spiritual factors or pure spirits that are behind such and such material phenomenon; they are capable of expiating such and such evil force or a blind and oppressive power from which they develop very general and explanatory cosmogonies and moral value systems.

However, in Africa, Gods, spirits, and supernatural powers have never been isolated from human preoccupations. They are embodied in natural totalities: animal or vegetal. They are anthropomorphic in their intentions and deeds. Human beings can kill them as in the popular African legend of *Ouagadou Bida*. As Modibo Sidibé (1999) tells it, the story takes place in eleventh-century Ghana but it is told in various African cultures: Ouagadou-Bida is a holy serpent spirit that lives in a Sacred Grove and protects the kingdoms. But legend requires a yearly sacrifice of a beautiful girl for the serpent to continue protecting the people. One year, a beautiful girl named Sia is the choice for sacrifice but she is engaged to a great warrior named Amadou Séfédokoté. Amadou gets upset about the sacrifice and decides to put an end to it. He hides behind a tree and waits for Ouagadou-Bida. When the serpent appears, Amadou cuts off its head, but Ouagadou-Bida grows another one. It was only after the seventh head that the spirit dies. Without the spirit to protect Ghana, legend has it that a drought falls across the Kingdom, killing crops and animals.

Thus, besides a hero's exploits, one can act on God with words, incantations, evocations, spells, conjurations, exorcisms, magical practices, songs, amulet charms, and works of art, meals, ritual feasts, or animal sacrifices. Africans act on the supreme forces to make them available. The Gods' existence is related to the idea of earth fertility, the sky, cattle, and the forest.

The effect of natural forces on Africans is a proof of their helplessness and limited power. The spirits or Negro African Gods among other things control lightning and precipitations. The Gods dispense rain, provide water to sources, and control scarcity and individual or collective abundance. Here, Gods are just propitiatory and exist to vitalize the earth. They are conceived insofar as they help to prevent or smooth away contradictions between fellow human beings, human beings and nature, and particularly acute contradictions in societies where human beings' material domination on nature is weaker, and where therefore, tools are reinforced by rites to make up for the limitations. Thus, the increasing number of "priest" activities and occult practices occur only when during failed harvests, starvations, epidemics, or after a lightning strike.

The witchcraft phenomenon is connected to the finding of a balance that is conformed to African social structures, while a myth in its content is the organization of natural elements that Africans have implemented or met in the course of their current lives. As for the moral categories, they are calls to material sobriety, mutual aid, or solidarity inside the productive unit governed by egalitarian economic rapports. Thus between these two levels of phenomena—the material and the spiritual—we are dealing with a necessary liaison in which the important aspect turns out to be the individual or collective life satisfied through human labor and the contact between humans, nature, and their peers whose exigencies call for mind creations, languages, and artworks.

However, these categories become an ideological praxis justifying the social hierarchy between nobles and slaves, nobles and "free" peasants, and "free" peasants and slaves. Therefore, in societies where agriculture and cattle breeding are the dominant activities, the perpetuation of political structures through chieftainships, kingdoms, or empires has served to safeguard the existing institutions. These formations plead in favor of an obvious relationship between matter and consciousness or "infrastructure" and "superstructure." As Marx puts it: "Thinking and being are thus certainly *distinct*, but at the same time they are in *unity* with each other" (93); or "Just as plants, animals, stones, air, light, etc., constitute theoretically a part of human consciousness" (67) and "Man makes his life activity itself the object of his will and his consciousness" (68).

Thus, spiritual manifestations, which are ideological elements, are inseparable from the exigencies of real life from which they stem. For Hegel—as well as for Plato with his kingdom of ideas and palpable essence of the world—reality is other than the level of objects or phenomena. Existence stems from the concept, the idea, or the self-generating, self-developing, and self-determining insular consciousness, which determines empirical reality. Negro African reality invalidates the absolutism of concepts, ideas, and categories. Here, there are no categories whose objective content does not have an empirical foundation and a concrete content, or the characteristics of a reality reproduced by abstraction.

We can now safely say that in traditional Africa, the head, otherwise known as the brain, is the seat, or the vehicle of thought, whose source—as we have mentioned earlier—is the concrete reality, nature, and the social environment. Besides the general connections and the relations of dependence we have shown, we can conclude—outside of any terminological prejudice—that the conditions of social existence and the social consciousness in turn form a unity or an "eco-

114   *Chapter Six*

nomic and social formation." This brings into perspective Marx's dear notion of "primitive communism." We can also understand why some Afrocentrist scholars and particularly John Henrik Clarke (1998) calls him "A Johnny come lately" in the sense that Marx's communist ideas had already been in existence in pre-colonial Africa.

Indeed, in the social and economic formation we have described, there are as many survivals of elements proper to a "primitive communism." They range from the egalitarian relationships of production, the importance of the beneficial kinship relations governing members of the same productive unit to the organization of collective hunting and gathering from time to time—despite the abundance of food producing provided by agriculture and cattle breeding in the Sahel—the verbal sanctions of exaggerations, the control and internalization of the other, the condemnation of selfishness, and any form of individualism. Today, many people in the equatorial forest live under these principles. However, among the nations where agriculture and cattle breeding have become predominant, the dominance of such principles has shrunk.

Slavery

Slavery as explained by Hegel has never existed in Africa. This is so even though Meillassoux's *Anthropology of Slavery* (1992) now finds that the variety and intensity of servile relationships and methods of oppression have flourished in Africa a very long time before the Europeans. The capitalist ideology is apologetic and at the same time, constantly adjusts its target. Therefore, and despite Meillassoux decent scholarship, we steer clear of any research exonerating European Arab mass deportation of enslaved human beings to build capital, or any blame-sharing theory of Africa's having started it first. For now, we choose to adopt the findings of the present majority of sources, which agrees on the total opposite of such theories. We have witnessed the effect of the theories of a guilty Africa on a number of people. Besides being part of the dominant ideology, it is a balm that soothes White people's guilt and many Black people's fear and resentment for being originally connected to Africa, the savage and dark continent. Now, we have not been able to find a term that would differentiate the types of bondage that has existed in Africa. Thus, for lack of a better term, we use "slave" and "slavery."

Contrary to Hegel's theses on slavery, slaves in Africa—and this without any value judgment—are more than anywhere else, integrated into social life. They are neither pushed aside nor reduced to mere means of production as in other slave regimes. Diagne says: "L'esclavage n'est pas comme dans le monde gréco-romain ou asiatique un pur rapport d'exploitation (Cf. sur ce point les status politique du Soudan nigérien; dans les civilisations d'Afrique centrale, dans celle des Yoruba, Ashanti ou des Sérères): l'esclavage a même longtemps rencontré un refus d'institutionalisation" [Slaves are not, as in the Greco-Roman or Asian world, a pure relation of exploitation (Cf. The political status Nigerian Sudan; Central African civilizations, among the Yoruba, Ashanti or Sérères): for a long time, the institutionalization of slavery has met fierce opposition] (24).

Diop, Davidson, Bohannan, Curtain, Turnbull, and most Africanists share our earlier description of Africa that we reiterate before offering a more up to date and materialist reading of African society: traditional African societies downplay isolation and individualism and emphasize communities based on strong family relationships. In these societies, all members are regarded as part of an extended family, making the selling of relatives unacceptable. Human bondage did exist in Africa, but it was a local serfdom, very different from the large-scale monopolized commerce of human beings. The purpose of the Arab and European system of slavery was to provide plantations, mines and factories with a forced and cheap labor.

Diagne's point is that human bondage in Africa was not primarily economic: it was primarily social and political. This is explained by the fact that "Political and economic rights are granted to all social categories no matter what order, cast, or corporation they belong to" (24). That is why slaves could move up into the ranks of free people. They were granted land (for life in many parts of Africa) to cultivate for their own use. They could marry other slaves, and their children would be free citizens. Slaves often occupied important positions in society. They were used in domestic, and also in political and military activities. However, as Diagne says, it appears that it is only with the advent of the Triangular Commerce, better known as the Atlantic slave trade—connected to the expansion of capitalism—that a neat systematization of slavery starts to take place in Africa; hence the apparition of slave merchants who later on oppose the abolition of slavery, their new source of interests. The historian J. D. Fage states: "There seems in fact to have been a close connection between economic development and the growth of slavery within West African society. The commercial revolutions initiated in Guinea by the Atlantic slave trade, and in the Sudan by the trans-Saharan trade, seem undoubtedly to have influenced the formation in West Africa of a new way . . . which approximated more closely to the idea of chattel slavery" (93).

Social Structures

The particularity of the African social and economic formation resides in the fact that the entire condition of existence does not rest on exclusive slave labor as in the case of the slave social and economic formation known to Western antiquity. The African system cannot be reduced to feudalism, which is characterized by lords' ownership over slaves that they can sell at will. It can neither be understood as a stage beyond "slavery." The persistence of some of its aspects is not a simple survival or the appearance of a new feudal formation whose normal development has been suppressed by European colonialism. Identifying it to either a social or economic formation would be illegitimate for the simple reason that in Africa, slavery has not experienced an era of full booming where the ultimate phase of its evolution would clear the way for a superior formation. It is a formation that identifies itself with the "Asian social condition of existence, which Marx and Engels mention regarding India and China and which, according to Jean Roux (1969) would be "caracterisé par des communautés villageoises, égalitaires, sans propriétés privées de la terre, mais dont le surplus de production était prélevé par une monarchie despotique qui, en contrepartie, entretient un system d'irrigation nécessaire sous le climat indien et qu'une seule communauté n'aurait pu entretenir à elle seule. Ainsi coexistait l'exploitation avec une égalité à la base" [characterized by egalitarian village communities with no private ownership of the land, but with a surplus production levied by a despotic monarchy. In turn, the monarchy maintains an irrigation system that is necessary under the Indian climate but unmanageable by a single community. That is how exploitation coexists with equality at the basis] (287).

It is also a condition in which there is acceleration of the political basis but not of the economic one. The sociologist Boubacar Ly (1977) explains that it is the case where the emergence of a state has not sprung from a class-stratified society; thus here, history is repetitive but not cumulative.

In traditional Africa, (1) even if several superstructures happen to overlap, they always manifest themselves within the limit set up by the social conditions of existence, the level of productive forces, and the nature of existence relations; (2) classes are classes of propriety in the sense that slaves, and to some extent "free" citizens, produce a "surplus-value" on domains that are not theirs. While in the Asian condition of social existence and according to Ly, "Il s'agit de la classe de fonction qui ont leur origine dans les fonctions assumées" [we are dealing with functioning classes that stem from their assumed functions]; 3) this social and economic formation is cautiously called pre-capitalist mode of production, or often daringly called African mode of production, lineage, feudal-tributary, or community-based. For a greater convenience, we prefer to call it servo-feudal conditions of social existence. In such a formation, history is not repetitive: there are bounds, qualitative changes in so far as we have admitted the hypothesis of an anterior "primitive communism" that is still visible. In traditional Africa thus, there is an internal dynamism which is the driving force of a history that can be considered "repetitive" or "stationary," only if viewed from the more rapid movement of Western societies since the Industrial Revolution.

Diagne explains that in fact, pre-Islamic and pre-colonial Black Africa—especially in less urbanized rural societies—was essentially based on "Une démocratie horizontale et non verticale, c'est à dire sous des formes populaires de pouvoir qui opèrent à travers des régimes et des systèmes legalistes, conservateurs et inégalitaristes. Elle exclut l'anarchie; elle est du côté de l'ordre; ce sera sa force et sa faiblesse peut-être" [A horizontal and not vertical democracy, meaning under popular forms of power operating through legalistic, conservative, and inegalitarian regimes and castes. It excludes anarchy and upholds order; this will be its strength and perhaps its weakness] (24).

The level of differentiation and structures of African societies can only explain such a social and political order. The analysis of such processes takes us back to the social and economic genesis of African states, more precisely, the centralized West African ones, for they are of great historical significance. They neatly indicate that traditional Africa never escaped from the reality of class antagonism, undermining Negritudinist positions. The opposition does not reside in the fact that the class of the rich does not have economic relations with the poor. On the contrary, those very relations are contradictory because they are based on exploitation and unequal interests. In fact, the practical process of differentiation and class opposition is revealed through the neater and neater inequality between the interests and concerned groups.

However, such an inequality, at least at the beginning, does not necessarily lead to obvious conflicts. Initially, it remains latent and can only be perceived in the will of concerned groups and in their efforts *to organize themselves in order to avoid anarchy*. At that time appear orders, castes, and finally a class as so many organic expressions of social inequality. The concerned groups try to institutionalize them, i.e., to give them a legal form and therefore make them acceptable for the entire society. However, this organization, because it necessarily stems from the initiative of groups in high positions and who want to preserve their own social benefits, cannot but reflect the interests of such groups. Even if such organization shows some form of harmony and collaboration among groups, it still expresses class antagonism—not yet visible—in its very principle. Pierre Fougeyrollas 9!974) tells us:

> Ainsi, sous la co-existence des ethnies de pasteurs et de paysans, sous la co-existence hiérarchisée des orders et des castes, les sociétés sahel-soudanaises ont connu le processus, latent ou manifeste, réprimé ou exacerbé, de la lutte des classes; le fait a été que de grandes familles nobles (sacerdotales et guerrières) ont contrôlé la production paysanne et pastorale. Même si l'ancien droit africain n'a pas généralement reconnu une propriété privée du sol et des troupeaux, la terre et le bétail ont été, en fait, à la disposition de quelques uns érigés par là en maîtres du plus grand nombre. [Thus, under the co-existence of ethnic shepherds and peasants, their hierarchized co-existence of orders and castes, Sahelo-Sudanese societies have experienced the latent or obvious, repressed or exacerbated process of class struggle; the fact has been that sacerdotal or warlike noble families have controlled peasant ant pastoral production. Even when traditional African laws in general do not consider lands and cattle private properties, they have remained, in fact, at the disposal of some people who set themselves up as masters of the majority]. (5)

What happens is that those very few, whose official functions are to divide the economic resources, have every time seized upon the surplus production, thus progressively detaching themselves from the productive masses. They gradually become a layer of privileged non-producers and consequently, constitute the state apparatus in Africa. As well explained by Dieng, this economic surplus—which is the state's objective foundation—is linked to the exploitation of the vast resources offered by the great rivers of Sénégal and Niger. Dieng shows how, in Africa,

> Les vallées alluviales du niger et du Sénégal ont permis l'existence, dans certaines regions, d'une double récolte qui donne naissance à un surplus économique susceptible d'engendrer une différenciation sociale. Leur vallées sont des zones favorables à l'élevage, à l'agriculture, à la pêche, à la chasse et à l'exercice de métiers artisanaux. Elles ont été des zones de contact entre populations à mode de vie different. C'est dans ces endroits que se sont développées les villes commerçantes de Gao, Tombouctou, Djenné, Silla, tékrour etc. [The alluvial valleys of Sénégal and Niger have favored, in certain areas, the existence of a double crop, which creates an economic surplus likely to engender social differentiations. These valleys are favorable zones for cattle breeding, agriculture, fishing, hunting, and the practice of craftsmanship. They have been contact zones between populations of various ways of life. The commercial cities of Gao, Timbuktu, Djenné, Silla, and Tekrur grew out of those very locations. (43-44).

Thus appears, maybe partially, African reality in its authenticity. What is proven is that Africa is not and has never been a static continent, impervious to the historic movement. Like other societies, it has experienced upward historical processes as explained by Diop's *Precolonial Black Africa* (2003) and *Anteriority of Negro Civilizations* (2003), which are ethnophilosophically oriented but offer in-depth research of the matter. Otherwise, we can retain the idea that Ancient Egypt—which has reached a very high level of development on all plans—was the original nucleus from which African societies are elaborated; and this, contrary to what Hegel has thought. Africa has also experienced regressive historical phases: the collapse of Egypt, the desertification of the once fertile and irrigated Sahara, the Atlantic slave trade and the capital accumulation of a nascent capitalist Europe, colonization and neo-colonization/globalization, which have given the continent its present profile.

In traditional African realities, such are—with a lesser ambiguity—the levels that we think are open to a dialectic, materialistic, and historic interpretation. They are also Marxist categories that we think can be universalized and applied to traditional Negro African realities. It is even more so in the "historic period" of Africa, in which social and economic formations are entangled. The capitalism that has created these categories in other climes exists in all African countries: a system of inequality, structured on the orientation of the production towards market demands and perpetuated by the division of society into rich and poor.

Is There an African Specificity?

Despite some certain and practical limitations and possible theoretical imperfections, we have arrived at the end of our conceptual itinerary. Does "traditional" Africa exist? Without beating around the bush, and contrary to all the anti-ethnophilosophical expectations, Paulin Hountondji (1996) summarizes by affirming that "traditional" Africa opposes its objectivity and resists any erasure by a simple conceptual decree. For Africans, culture equals identity. However, this identity is not individual but rather communal, a common history and a common heritage. It is this aspect of the ancestral ties that unites a people, which is very different from the separate and hierarchical identity that exists in the Western world. Now, does "traditional" Africa offer "a universal face" to the world? Based on impartial and scientific observations, the answer is affirmative. We have found that Hountondji's anti-ethnophilosophy seems to fall into some kind of empiricism, seeing African societies only as given phenomena, concrete objects or particular individualities. As for Kwame Nkrumah's rigorous typology from his *Conscienscism* (1970), it shares the same theoretical background with ethnophilosophy. Both positions are caught within the limits of the political struggle of the time, mandated by a strong culturalism. They limit their analysis, not to African societies in their concrete manifestation, but wrongly, to the exclusive affirmation of the specificity, originality, or unique traits common to all African societies.

For us, African reality is no longer to be viewed as an ensemble of monads without any relation with each other and the rest of the world. Indeed, with an effort of speculative abstraction, scholars have relied on sensual testimonies to conclude that there is an irreducible diversity in African societies. Another abstraction no less speculative has further pushed the analysis to limit it to the only traits that are similar to these societies. However, pursuing the investigation all the way reveals that an African society and the entire African culture as a singularity possess important proprieties linking them to one another and also to other human societies. This goes to the credit of anti-ethnophilosophy and to some extent, Senghor's "Civilization of the Universal" develops the same idea: the particular become exalted and, thus, contributes to the many convergent but multiple civilizations of the universal.

It is generally admitted that content proper is not incompatible with the general. Particularities are subsumed in the general. In dialectic terms, the particular and the general characterize the same and only object. Particularities are what fill the universal. That is, the general exists through the particular and the particular belongs to the general. In the Negro universe, the universal is reflected, among other concepts, by the dialectic concepts of Hegel and Marx. Only the categories of historical materialism are likely to reflect that dialectic of the particular and the general and the very universal itself, which has been so far occulted by metaphysics and relativism.

From the critical examinations of Charles Darwin's, Lewis H. Morgan's, Marx's and Engels's works, Emmanuel Terray (1972) underlines the following: "[In Africa as well as elsewhere], it makes it futile to use man's 'mental achievements to argue that there is a difference in kind between the biological and the spiritual, between the animal and the human' . . . to admit a discontinuity between the animal kingdom and the human kingdom: . . . the frontier between humanity and the animal no longer occurred within the human species . . . for it was a unity, both in time and space" (14-15).

We agree with Feuerbach's principal understanding of the unity of mind and body "the brain cannot be formed without phosphorous-bearing fat . . . Without phosphorous, no thought" (70). Thus, the spirit would be the thinking phosphorus in ourselves. However, we only subscribe to this thesis as long as it integrates new dimensions in its conception of human beings and reconciles around it the physical materiality—the individual in flesh and blood as a raw product, unchanged in its nature—with the biological, the social, and history, and agrees with Marx's Thesis VI of *Theses on Feuerbach* (1845): "The human essence is no abstraction inherent in each single individual. In its reality, it is the ensemble of the social relations" (145).

The categories that we have just explored—Negro African thought, the sphere of activities—economy, human, nature, slavery, class, and society—are just but a few examples illustrating the unity and originality of Negro African cultures. The originality of these realities does not limit itself to such domains. It also verifies itself at the level of facts and institutions that are as varied as market, parenthood, totemic problems, architectures, hairstyle, and so forth.

Epilogue

The description of labor in traditional Africa is equal to the one among the Trobriand Islanders, which Bronislaw Malinowski gives in his *Argonauts of the Western Pacific: An Account of Native Enterprise and Adventure of the Archipelagoes of Melanesian New Guinea* (1922). For these societies, everything is an opportunity to communicate, to have conversation, to sing, to dance, to exchange, and the whole thing is done in public and for publicity's sake. They not only practice their humanity but they also show off that practice: human beings exchanging and communicating for the sake of doing so.

Hegel seizes reality as a unity: the unity of what exists and the appearance of what exists. Things are around a long time before people realize that they exist. Hegel places himself at the heart of modern political economy. He conceives labor as the essence and confirmation of the human essence. Hegel is right: nature is a moment of the development of the Idea, human conscious activity, or the moment when that conscious activity becomes unconscious; when thought and activity—proper to human beings—become the propriety of things as they imitate human beings. Therefore, nature is indeed an imitation of the Idea.

Experts have studied primitive, archaic, savage societies or developing countries but so far, concerns and findings remain in love with the primitive, small, and unsophisticated. However, as long as we perceive these people as children of nature, unconscious and lazy, who avoid as much as possible any hard and painstaking activities—just waiting for some ripe fruit to fall off trees—we remain mistaken and unable to seize the *motivations* behind any community undertakings. On the contrary and in truth, they can work harshly and effectively and in a systematic manner. Suffice it to read a few pages from Malinowski or Elungu to understand that the motivation for labor in the so-called archaic societies is apodictic happiness—the pure pleasure of suppressing labor or practicing exchange and publicity.

Current views on the primitive *Homo economicus* portray him as an indolent, individualist, and carefree being that is at the same time logical and consequent in his behavior, guided by strictly utilitarian motivations. Another error, inherent to the one above, believes that savages can only conceive very simple forms of simple labors, without method or organization. There is yet another sophism on primitive economies—more or less explicitly formulated in all the literature of these times—which consists in the belief that primitive people have only rudimentary forms of commerce and exchange at their disposal; that these forms play only an inessential role in the tribe's existence, only by jolts every now and then when necessity knows no law, and that exchange disappears as suddenly as it has appeared. It can also be about the popular illusion of a primitive Golden Age—mostly characterized by the absence of any distinction between yours and mine—and the more precious idea of the existence of stages when a human being looks for food all by himself or herself and isolates families providing for their needs. Numerous theories see in primitive economies only a simple search for a means of existence.

Modern anthropology—in the works of Jacques Cauvin (1978) and Marshall Sahlins (1980)—has ceaselessly ruined all these theories and has proven that any tribal life rests on a continuous exchange *system* of material goods. Moreover, modern archeology, always inspired by ethnography, shows how commerce, going from the simple exchange of goods to a neatly more complex system, has been an important agent of social transformation, and how it has paved the way for the centralized economies of Cnossos and Mycenae, the cradles of modern publicity.

The idea that contemporary Neolithic human beings can live at the stage of individual food search or isolating family supplies means that we are dealing with reformist, asocial, and cold calculating beings; thus, human beings are only capable of an enjoyment confined to things themselves. Such a conception ignores the profound feeling of publicity, which drives people to display what they own and to share and give away. To exchange for exchange's sake constitutes one of the essential characteristics that ethnography reveals; and the universal and fundamental nature of this practice allows us to put forward that it is a common trait to all primitive societies.

We have one last sophism according to which archaic savages keep in their possession everything that they need and do not give it away to anyone on their own free will. Such an understanding seems to better fit modern individuals. It does not mean that savages are not strongly inclined to keep what they own. On the contrary, it is because they attach so much importance to the fact of giving away that the distinction between yours and mine is reinforced rather than effaced.

Some Truth on Thirdworldism

Underdevelopment is indeed an acculturation, but not of the periphery by the center but of the center by the periphery. The center represents the developed or industrialized nations and the periphery the developing or poorer ones. This is only possible because the so-called economic development is not economic but pure culture and communication. The acculturation of the center by the periphery is obviously not the center's doing but the *principle* of the periphery: fetishism. It is this fetishism, which is only been ritual, dreamed of, wished, and invoked in Paris, London, Tokyo, and New York. Therefore, if there is acculturation, it is not of Africa by Europe or America but definitely of Europe and America by the *African principle* of society, which happens to be a universal one. The world is fetishist; therefore, the world is African.

Thus, what passes for acculturation of Africa by the so-called developed nations today is only the return of the now fully developed African principle of fetishism back to the country. We are talking about the principle that peasants have welcomed with open arms and for which they have abandoned their lands—not because of any misery but on their own free will—to rejoin the city where the principles that they have always revered are celebrated in full scale. However, it is also pure Hegelian understanding: yes, Africa has been kept outside of history like some kind of museum of the original principle of alienation, which is fetishism. Indeed, the foundation appears to be a regression, a return toward the original and true, or toward what has taken the place of a beginning. The accomplished fetishism has returned to Africa.

There is indeed an attempt of acculturation of the periphery by the center but not as commonly understood. The center in itself is made up by the total triumph of the African principle of the mana (the power of things), the fantastic, and the alienation of communication. Now we have a better idea about why the dominant ideology must conceal the triumph of a savage Negro principle. What the center and its dominant ideology want to occult at all cost is its *proper Negritudinization*. Therefore, there is indeed a struggle for the periphery to "deculturalize" countries whose cultures are in fact perfectly apt to understand the return of the fetishism or mana. Who else is better situated than Africa and Africans to understand the total Africanization of the so-called developed countries? Their Africanization is exactly what has really been developed in such countries.

However, the thing in-itself, which is returning to Africa—fetishism developed by 2,000 years of history, commerce, merchandise, capital, and money—is not acculturating for the periphery. That explains why it is successful among the peasants of the periphery. If we want to talk about underdevelopment in Africa, it can only be an underdevelopment of the mana: in Europe, America, or Japan, the mana is much more developed than in Africa. If we try to find a term for the return of this developed fetishism to the country, we must talk about *surculturalization* and not acculturation.

What savages see coming to them on the merchant ships is what they themselves are but only developing after 2,000 years of adventures. That is how one can explain the enthusiasm European explorers have met when they brought their shoddy goods on the shores of Africa. European merchants have taken Africans for imbeciles while Africans have understood the nature of merchandise better than them. Africans have seen arriving on the European vessels their proper nature explained or revealed by 2,000 years of Odyssey.

Hegel says: "What is rational is actual and what is actual is rational" (10). We say: "What is magical is rational and what is rational is magical because the magical is the rational that does not know itself yet."

Bibliography

Abiodun, Rowland. "African Aesthetics." *Journal of Aesthetic Education 35*, no. 4 (Winter, 2001).
Alexandre, Pierre. *Languages and Language in Black Africa*. Evanston, IL: NorthwesternUniversity Press, 1972.
Appiah, Kwame. *In My Father's House: Africa in the Philosophy of Culture*. New York: Oxford University Press, 1992.
Avinieri, Shlomo. *Hegel's Theory of the Modern State*. Cambridge: Cambridge University Press, 1972.
Ba, Diadie. "Africans Still Seething Over Sarkozy Speech." September 2007. http://uk.reuters.com/article/idUKL0513034620070905 (accessed January 2010).
Bâ, Amadou Hampaté. *Aspects de la civilization africaine*. Paris: Présence Africaine, 1972.
Ben-Amos, Paula Girshick. *The Art of Benin*. Washington, DC: The Smithsonian Institute, 1995.
Bonetto, Sandra. "Hegel, Race, and Racism: An Analysis." *Minerva: An Internet Journal of Philosophy*. Volume 10, 2006.
Buck-Morss, Susan. *Hegel, Haiti, and Universal History*. Pittsburgh, PA: University of Pittsburgh Press, 2009.
Burns, Tony. *Natural Law and Political Ideology in the Philosophy of Hegel*. Brookfield, VT: Ashgate Publishing Company, 1996.
Carstens, Vicki and Frederick Parkinson, eds. *Advances in African Linguistics*. Trenton,NJ: Africa World Press, Inc, 2000.
Cauvin, Jacques. *Les premiers villages de Syrie-Palestine du IXe au XIIe millenaire avant Jésus Christ.Travaux de la Maison de l'Orient 4, série archaéologique 3*. Lyons, France: Maison de l'Orient, 1978.
Césaire, Aimé. *Discourse on Colonialism*. New York: Monthly Review Press, 2000.
Cieszkowski, August von. *Prolégomènes à l'historiosophie*. Paris: Editions Champ Libre, 1973.
Childs, Tucker George. *An Introduction to African Languages*. Philadelphia: John Benjamin Publishing Company, 2003.
Clarke, John Henrik. *John Henrik Clarke: A Great Mighty Walk*, 1998.
Colloque sur la littérature et l'esthétique négro-africaines. Abidjan, Dakar, Lomé: Nouvelles Editions Africaines, 1979.

Coquery-Vidrovitch, Catherine. *Africa: Endurance and Change South of the Sahara.* Berkeley, CA: University of California Press, 1988.

Denis, Henri. *L' "Economie" de Marx: histoire d'un échec.* Paris: Presses Universitaires de France, 1992.

Diagne, Pathé. "De la démocratie traditionnelle." *Présence Africaine*, 1976.

———. *Formations sociales et commerce à longue distance en Afrique de l'ouest.* Dakar: Sankoré, 1975.

Dieng, Amady Aly. *Contribution à l'étude des problèmes philosophiques en Afrique Noire.* Dakar: Nubia-Sankoré, 1983.

———. *Hegel, Marx et Engels et les problèmes de l'Afrique noire.* Dakar: Editions Sankoré, 1978.

———. *Le marxisme et l'Afrique noire.* Dakar: Nubia-Sankoré, 1986.

Dietzgen, Josef. *L'essence du travail intellectuel humain. Préface de Anton Pannekoek.* Paris: Editions Champ Libre, 1973.

Diop, Cheikh Anta. *The African Origin of Civilization.* Westport, CT: Lawrence Hill, 2003.

———. *Civilisation ou Barbarie: anthropologie sans complaisance.* Paris: Présence Africaine, 1981.

———. *Pre-colonial Black Africa.* Westport, CT: Lawrence Hill, 2003.

Eliade, Mircea. *Mythes, Dreams, and Mysteries: the Encounter Between Contemporary Faiths and Archaic Realities.* New York: HarperCollins, 1979.

Elungu, P. E. A. *Tradition africaine et rationalité moderne.* Paris: L'harmattan, 1987.

Fanon, Frantz. *Black Skin White Masks.* New York: Grove Press, 1967.

Feuerbach, Ludwig. *Principles of the Philosophy of the Future.* Hackett Publishing Company, 1986.

Forbes, Duncan. "Introduction." *Lectures on the Philosophy of World History*, 1975.

Fougeyrollas, Pierre, "Défi de la sécheresse et lutte en Afrique soudano-sahélienne." Paper presented at the *Séminaire sur l'environnement et le développement économique dans les zones arides et sub-arides*, Niamey, Niger, February-March 1974.

Franco, Paul. *Hegel's Philosophy of Freedom.* New Haven, CT: Yale University Press, 1999.

Freud, Sigmund. *Civilization and Its Discontents.* New York: W. W. Norton: 1961.

Gans, Gerald and Chanran Kukathas, eds. *Handbook of Political Theory.* Thousand Oaks, CA: Sage, 2004.

Gendzier, Irene L. *Frantz Fanon: A Critical Study.* New York, Pantheon, 1973.

Gobineau, Joseph Arthur Comte de. *Essai sur l'inégalité des races*, 5e ed. Paris: Librairie de Paris, 1853.

———. *The Inequality of Human Races.* New York: Howard Fertig, 1967.

Godelier, Maurice. *La notion de 'mode de production asiatique' et les schéma marxistes d'évolution des sociétés.* Paris: Centre d'Etude et de Recherche Marxistes, 1975.

Gordon, Lewis Ricardo. *An Introduction to Africana Philosophy.* Cambridge: Cambridge University Press, 2008.

Gouliane, G. I. *Hegel ou la philosophie de la crise.* Paris: Payot, 1970.

Grinker, Roy Richard and Christopher B. Steiner, eds. "Research on an African Mode of Production." *Perspectives on Africa: a Reader in Culture, History, and Representation.* Cambridge, MA: Blackwell, 1997.

Hegel, Georg Wilhelm Friedrich. *Early Theological Writings.* Chicago, IL: University of Chicago, 1975

———. *Aesthetics: Lectures on Fine Art, Volume I*. Translated by T. M. Knox. London: Oxford University Press, 1975.

———. *Lectures on the Philosophy of Religion, Together with a Work on the Proofs of the Existence of God, Volume II*. Translated by the Rev. E. B. Speirs, B. D. and J. Burdon Sanderson. New York: Humanities Press Inc., 1968.

———. *Lectures on the Philosophy of World History*. Translated by H. B. Nisbet. New York: Cambridge University Press, 1984.

———. *The Philosophy of History*. Translated by J. Sibree. Buffalo, New York: Prometheus Books, 1991.

———. *Philosophy of Mind: Being Part Three of the Encyclopaedia of the Philosophical Sciences (1830)*. Tranlated by William Wallace. Cambridge: Cambridge University Press, 1971.

———. *The Philosophy of History*. New York, NY: Dover, 1956.

———. *The Philosophy of Right*. Translated by T. M. Knox. London: Oxford University Press, 1967.

———. *La raison dans l'histoire*. Translated by Kostas Papaioannou. Paris: 10/18, 2007.

———. *Science of Logic*. Translated by A. V. Miller. Atlantic Highlands, NJ: Humanities Press International, Inc., 1989.

———. *Science de la logique II*. Translated by Vladimir Yankelevitch. Paris: Aubier, 1947.

Heine, Bernd and Nurse, Derek. *African Languages: An Introduction*. London: Cambridge University Press, 2000.

Hobbes, Thomas. *Leviathan, Part 1 & 2*. Toronto: Broadview Editions, 2005.

Holy Bible: The New American Bible. Wichita, Kansas: Fireside Bible Publishers, 2001.

Hondt, Jacques d'. *Hegel in his time*. Lewinston, New York: Broadview Press, 1988.

Hountondji, Paulin J. *African Philosophy: Myth & Reality*. Bloomington, IN: IUP, 1996.

Hyppolite, Jean. *Genesis and Structure of Hegel's Phenomenology of Spirit*. Evanston, IL: Northwestern University Press, 1974.

———. *Logic and Existence*. New York: SUNY Press, 1997.

Jahn, Janheinz. *Muntu: the New African Culture*. New York: Grove Press, 1991

———. *Liberté 1: Négritude et humanisme*. Paris: Seuil, 1984.

———. *Liberté 3: Négritude et Civilization de l'universel*. Paris: Seuil, 1977.

———. *Prose and Poetry*. Selected and translated by John Reed and Clive Wake. London, OUP, 1965.

Jowett, Benjamin. *Protagoras*. http://www.mlahanas.de/Greeks/Texts/Plato/Protagoras. Html (accessed June 1, 2010).

Kamdem, Emmanuel. "Temps et travail en Afrique." *L'individu dans l'organization: les dimensions oubliées*, 8e ed.. Jean-François Chanlat, ed. Québec: Editions ESKA, 2007.

Kant, Immanuel. *Critique of Pure Reason*. London: Penguin Books, 2008.

Kenyatta, Jomo. *Facing Mount Kenya: the Tribal Life of Gikuyu*. New York: Vintage Books, 1962.

Kojève, Alexandre. *Introduction to the Reading of Hegel: Lectures on the Phenomenology of Spirit*. New York: Cornell University Press, 1980.

Levy-Bruhl, Lucien. *How Natives Think*. New York: Alfred K. Knopf, 1926.

Longuenesse, Béatrice. *Hegel's Critiques of Metaphysics*. New York: Cambridge University Press, 2007.

Ly, Boubacar. "Approches fondamentaux des sociétés africaines." Cours de sociologie en année de maîtrise de philosophie. Université Cheikh A. Diop. Dakar, Sénégal, 1976-1977.

Malinowski, Bronislaw. *Sex and Repression in Savage Societies*. London: Routledge, 2001.

Malson, Lucien and Itard, Jean. *Wolf Children*. New York: New Left Books, 1976.

Maquet, Jacques. *Africanity: The Cultural Unity of Black Africa*. New York: Oxford University Press, 1972.

———. *Civilization of Black Africa*. New York: Oxford University Press, 1972.

Marcuse, Herbert. *Reason and Revolution: Hegel and the Rise of Social Theory*. 2nd Ed. New York: Humanities Press, 1963.

Martinet, André. *Elements of General Linguistics*. Chicago: University of Chicago Press, 1982.

Marx, Karl. *Economic and Philosophic Manuscripts of 1844*. Moscow: Progress Publishers, 1985.

———. *Capital Unabridged. Vol. I: A Critical Analysis of Capitalist Production*. New York: International Publishers, 1992.

———. "German Ideology:" *Selected Works, Vol. I*. Moscow: Progress, 1983.

———. "Grundisse." *Marx-Engels Reader*. Robert W. Tucker, ed. New York: Norton, 1980.

———. "German Ideology." Tucker, 1978.

———. "On the Jewish Question." Tucker, 1978.

———. *La sainte famille*. Paris: Editions sociales, 1969.

———. "Theses on Feuerbach." Tucker, 1978.

Mbembé, Achille. "A Critique of Nicolas Sarkozy." africaresource.com_/index .php?option=com_content&crew (accessed June 10, 2010).

McCarney, Joseph, *Hegel on History*. London: Routledge, 2000.

Meillassoux, Claude. *L'anthropologie économique chez les Gouro de Côte d'Ivoire: de l'économie de subsistence à l'agriculture commerciale*. Paris: Mouton, 1964.

———. *The Anthropology of Slavery: The Womb of Iron and Gold*. Chicago: University of Chicago Press, 1992.

Mouelle, Ebenezer Njoh. *Jalon II: L'africanisme aujourd'hui*. Yaoundé: Editions CLE, 1975.

Najman, Charles. *Haiti: The End of the Chimères*, 2004.

Ndaw, Alassane. "La conscience esthétique Négro-africaine." *Art Nègre et civilization de l'universel*. Dakar: Nouvelles Editions Africaines, 1975.

——— "Formes du savoir dans la pensée traditionnelle." Philosophy lectures for M.A. degree offered at the University Cheikh A. Diop, Dakar, Senegal, 1976-1977.

———. *La pensée africaine: recherche sur les fondements de la pensée négro-africaine*. Dakar: Nouvelles Editions Africaines, 1983.

Nkrumah, Kwame. *Consciencism: Philosophy and Ideology for De-colonization*. New York: Monthly Review,1970.

Papaioannou, Kostas. *Marx et les marxistes*. Paris: Gallimard, 2001.

Pironet, Olivier. "Le philosophe et le president: une certaine vision." *Le Monde diplomatique* (November 2007).

Quillet, Pierre. "Hegel et l'Afrique." *Ethiopiques* no. 6 (Avril 1976).

Rousseau, Jean-Jacques. *The Social Contract, and the First and Second Discourses*. New Haven, CT: Yale University Press, 2002.

Roux, Jean. *Précis historique et théorique du marxisme-léninisme*. Paris: Robert Laffont, 1961.

Sahlins, Marshall David. *Au Coeur des sociétés: raison utilitaire et raison culturel*. Paris: Gallimard, 1980.

Samir Amin. *Accumulation on the World Scale: A Critique of the Theory of Underdevelopment*. New York: Monthly Review Press, 1978.

Sarkozy, Nicolas. "Discours du Président de la République Française à l'Université de Dakar, Sénégal," July 2007. http://www.elysee.fr/download (accessed January 2010).

Senghor, Léopold Sédar. "L'esthétique négro-africaine." *Diogène 16*. Paris: Gallimard, 1956.

———. *Les Fondements de l'africanité ou Négritude et arabité*. Paris: Présence Africaine, 1967.

———. *Liberté 1: Négritude et humanisme*. Paris: Seuil, 1984.

———. *Liberté 3: Négritude et Civilization de l'universel*. Paris: Seuil, 1977.

Shields, Allan. "Is There a Black Aesthetics?" *Leonardo 6*, no. 4 (Autumn 1973).

Sidibé, Modibo. *Legend of Ougadou-Bida*. Paris: Editions Donniya, 1999.

Société Africaine de Culture (SAP). "Des questions de méthodologie en esthétique." Semaine technique sur la réforme de l'enseignement de la philosophie, Dakar, Senegal, (March 28-30, 1977), 2.

Stace, Walter T. *The Philosophy of Hegel*. Carl J. Friedrich ed. New York: Modern Library Books, 1954.

Tavares, Franklin Pierre. "Hegel, critique de l'Afrique. Introduction aux etudes critiques de Hegel sur l'Afrique." Ph.D. Thesis. Univérsité de Paris I, 1990.

———. "Hegel et l'abbé Grégoire. Question noire et révolution française." *Annales historiques de la Révolution française* 3, no. 3 et 4 (1993).

———. "Hegel ou le silence sur Saint-Domingue in 1791-1991: Qui a peur de la démocratie en Haiti?" *Chemins critiques: revue haitiano-caraibéenne* 2, no. 2, Port-au-Prince, Haiti (Mai 1992).

———. "Hegel, philosophe anti-esclavagiste ou le jeune Hegel, lecteur de l'Abbé Raynal," conference au Collège de France (19 Janvier 1998).

Tempels, Placide. *La philosophie bantoue*. Paris: Présence Africaine, 1949.

———. *Bantu Philosophy*. Paris: Présence Africaine, 1959.

Terray, Emmanuel. *Marxism and Primitive Societies: Two Studies*. New York: Monthly Review, 1972.

Thompson, Robert Farris. "Yoruba Artistic Criticism." *The Traditional Artist in African Societies*. Bloomington: Indiana University Press, 1997.

Vogel, Susan Mullin. "African Art Western Eyes." *African Arts* 30, no 4. Special Issue: The Benin Centenary, Part 2 (Autumn 1997).

Wingo, Ajumé H. "The Many-Layered Aesthetics of African Art." *A Companion to African Philosophy*. Kwasi Wiredu, ed. Oxford: Blackwell Publishing Ltd, 2004.

Wole, Soyinka. "Colloque sur la littérature et l'esthétique négro-africaines." *Research in African Literatures* 14, no. 4 (Winter 1983) 562.

Yartseva, Viktoria. "Les universaux en tant que base de classification des langues." *Sciences Sociales* no.1. Paris: Académie des Sciences de l'URSS, 1975.

———. "Typology of Languages and the Problem of Universals." *Theoretical Aspects of Linguistics*. Moscow: USSR Academy of Sciences, 1977.

Index

Abidjan, 69, 71
Abiodun, Rowland, 71
Absolute spirit, 4, 5, 6, 8, 10, 11, 21, 31, 32, 34, 35, 51, 65
Absolute knowledge, 73, 84
Abstraction, 10, 47, 54, 57, 76, 77, 92, 113, 119, 120
Acculturation, 122, 123
Accumulation, 61, 73, 118
Adam & Eve, 81
aesthetics, 68, 69, 70, 73
Africanity, xii
Africanization, 121
African Portuguese, 72
agriculture, 7, 37, 38, 113, 114, 118
Alexandre, Pierre, 76
alienation, xviii, 3, 8, 13, 18, 43, 49, 56, 57, 60, 90, 91, 92, 93, 94, 96, 97, 99, 100, 103
alternative, 67, 100
America, 8, 21, 32, 38, 63, 109, 121
Amin, Samir, 61
antagonism, xvi, 28, 53, 60, 61, 117
anthropophagy, 18
appearance, 4, 24, 25, 63, 73, 115, 119
Appiah, Kwame Anthony, 75
appropriation, 55, 82, 107
arbitrariness, 12, 15, 19, 20
aristocracy, 112
Aristotle, ix, 6, 27, 69
artwork, 70, 71, 113
Ashanti, 17, 114, 115

Asia, 8, 32, 35, 38, 42
atheism, 14
Atlantic slave trade, 115, 118
Aufhebung, 84
Austria, 54
Bâ, Amadou Ampate, 78
Ba, Diadié, 32
Bantu, 28, 29, 30, 66, 69, 77
Benin plate, 72
Bernasconi, Robert, 22
Bohannan, Paul, xv, 115
Bonetto, Sandra, 22
bourgeoisie, 52, 54, 56, 58, 61
Buck-Morss, Susan, 86, 97, 98, 99, 100, 101
capitalism, xvii, 63, 109, 115
Cauvin, Jacques, 120
Césaire, Aimé, 21, 27, 29, 30
childhood, 8, 20, 40, 81
children, 3, 12, 19, 105, 115, 119
Childs, George Tucker, 74, 77
China, 7, 109, 116
Christianity, 53
Cieszkowski, August von, 101
circulation, 62, 110
city-state, xv, 50, 64
civil society, 43, 51, 53, 54, 55, 56, 57, 58, 59, 60, 92, 93, 94, 96
Clarke, John Henrik, xv, 114
class, 7, 52, 53, 54, 55, 56, 57, 58, 60, 61, 93, 99, 104, 116, 117, 120
climate, 5, 6, 7, 10, 32, 34, 36, 37, 116

Cnossos, 122
colluvies, 42
colonization, xv, xvii, 118
commerce, xvii, 61, 62, 63, 64, 115, 120, 121
communication, 26, 68, 75
concrete universal, 3, 9, 10, 11, 47, 56
condition of existence, 55, 113, 115, 116
Congo, xv, xvi, 27, 30
consciousness, 3, 4, 5, 7, 8, 9, 10, 13, 14, 16, 17, 18, 19, 20, 24, 28, 35, 41, 49, 59, 66, 68, 70, 71, 80, 81, 82, 84, 85, 86, 87, 88, 89, 90, 96, 98, 111, 112, 113
constitution, 9, 19, 39, 55, 59, 74
Coquery-Vidrovitch, Catherine, 61, 62, 109
Cornell, West, 45
cosmogony, 25
crystallization, 44, 47, 75, 109
culturalism, 119
Curtin, Phillip, xv
D'hondt, Charles, xv
Darwin, Charles, 120,
Davidson, Basil, 115
death, 15, 16, 17, 22, 81, 88, 89, 101, 104, 107, 108, 109
dehumanization, 93, 106
deification, 80
democracy, 59, 116
Democratic Republic of Congo, xvi
Dennis, Henri, 96, 97
desertification, 34, 38, 11
despotism, 10, 19, 20
determination, 7, 11, 34, 35, 36, 51, 61, 72, 84, 88
determinism, 6, 32, 36, 38
Dewey, John, 21
Dieng, Amady Aly, ix, xii, xv, 22, 27, 42, 62, 117, 118
Diagne, Pathé, 74, 114, 115, 116
Dietzgen, Josef, ix
Diop, Alioune, 27
Diop, Cheikh Anta, xv, 74, 75, 109, 110, 114, 118
DuBois, 21
Duncan, Forbes, 60

Egypt, 7, 20, 42, 78, 118
Eliade, Mircea, 67
Elungu, P.E.A., 103, 104, 105, 106, 119
emancipation, 59, 86
emotion, 22, 23, 24, 25, 52
empiricism, 34, 35, 44, 55, 119
Engels, Frederick, 61, 63, 116, 120
enlightenment, 52, 86, 100
equality, 42, 49, 50, 55, 116
Eritrean-Ethiopian War, xvi
essence, ix, 2, 7, 8, 14, 24, 28, 33, 35, 36, 39, 44, 45, 48, 50, 55, 57, 71, 80, 81, 85, 91, 92, 113, 120, 121
ethnography, 122
ethnophilosophy, 119
Eurocentrism, 16
exchange, 62, 96, 112, 121, 122
exploitation, xi, xvii, 32, 62, 114, 115, 116, 117, 118
exteriorization, 91, 93
Fage, J. D., 115
fanaticism, 17
Fanon, Franz, 96
fetish, 14, 15
fetishism, 123
feudalism, xvii, 115
Feuerbach, Ludwig, 100, 120, 9, 45
Fichte, ix,
Firmin, Antenor, 21
fluctuation, 20, 23
Fougeyrollas, Pierre, 37, 38, 117
France, 53, 91
Franco, Paul, 45, 48
freedom, xi, xii, 2, 3, 4, 5, 6, 8, 11, 18, 30, 41, 43, 45, 46, 47, 48, 49, 50, 51, 52, 53, 54, 55, 56, 57, 58, 59, 60, 61, 66, 70, 73, 81, 82, 84, 91, 92, 97, 99, 100
French Revolution, 49, 52, 53
Freud, Sigmund, 73, 94, 95
Ganges, 7
Garaudy, Roger, 53
geography, 5, 6, 7, 32, 34, 36
German Nation, 10, 35, 54
Germanic World, 10, 11, 42
Ghana, xv, 61, 112
Gikuyu, 107, 109

Girshick, Paula Ben-Amos, 72
globalization, xv, 118
Gobineau, Arthur Conte de, 22, 23
Godelier, Maurice, 61
Golden Age, 122
Gordon, Lewis, 21
Gouliane, G.I., 73
Gouro, 108
Green March, xvi
Haiti, 86, 97, 98, 99
Haitian Revolution, 86, 99
Haller, Carl Ludwig von, 45, 46
Hamite, 74
Heidegger, Martin, 110
Herodotus, 14
Hobbes, Thomas, 43, 44
homo economicus, 121
Hountondji, Paulin, 119
Humanity, xii, 1, 11, 12, 13, 20, 29, 39, 40, 42, 81, 84, 97, 98, 120, 121
Hyppolyte, Jean, 84, 98
Ibn Battuta, xv
Ibn khaldun, xv
Idea, the, 3, 6, 28, 36, 47, 48, 49, 51, 54, 55, 58, 61, 73, 121
idealism, 1, 24, 35, 52, 54, 60, 93, 97
immediacy, 3, 10, 23, 34
imperialism, xv, xvii, 32
individuality, 3, 4, 5, 7, 8, 87
Indus, 7
irrationality, 44, 49
Islam, 10, 21
Itard, Jean, 40
Ivory Coast, 108
Jahn, Janheinz, 78
James, CLR, 21
Jowette, Benjamin, 83
Kamdem, Emmanuel, xiii, 103, 106
Kant, Immanuel, ix, 1, 2, 21, 69
Kenyatta, Jomo
Knox, Robert, 22
Kojève, Alexandre, 86, 89
Latin alphabet, 76
Levy-Bruhl, Lucien, 24, 25, 26, 27, 28
Liberation, xvi, 3, 11, 17, 18, 82, 90, 91
Longuenesse, Beatrice, 2

Lordship and Bondage, 98, 100
Love, 12, 17, 73, 87, 88, 121
Ly, Boubacar, 116
Makeba, Miriam, 77
Mali, xv, 61
Malinowski, Bronislaw, 67, 121
Malson, Lucien, 40
mana, 123
Maquet, Jacques, 66, 75
Marcuse, Herbert, 79
Marx, Karl, ix, x, xvii, xviii, 21, 40, 43, 54, 55, 56, 57, 58, 59, 60, 61, 62, 63, 80, 85, 90, 91, 92, 93, 94, 95, 96, 98, 99, 100, 101, 103, 104, 107, 111, 113, 114, 116, 119, 120
master-slave dialectic, 86, 96
materialization, 47, 59
Mauritania, xvi
MBembe, Achille, 32
McCarney, Joseph, 41, 42
mechanization, 53, 93
Meillassoux, Claude, 107, 108, 114
merchandise, xvi, 63, 96, 123
metaphysics, 1, 29, 111, 119
Middle Ages, xv, 45
monarchy, 59, 116
money, xvi, 63, 96
Monomotapa, xv
Morgan, Lewis, 120
Morocco, xvi
motivations, 121, 122
Mycenae, 122
mystification, 55, 57, 58, 98
myth, 25, 66, 67, 81, 83, 99, 107, 113
Najman, Charles, 99
Napoleon, 53, 54
naturalness, 4, 5, 12, 16, 18, 39, 81, 82
Ndaw, Alassane, 67, 68, 70, 71
negation, 2, 35, 81, 84, 92, 100
negativity, 3, 18, 81, 87, 92
Negritude, 22, 23, 27, 71
Negritudinization, 123
Niger, xvi, 67, 118
Niger Movement for Justice, xvi
Nile, 7
Njoh-Mouelle, Ebenezer, 76
Nkrumah, Kwame, 78, 119

objectivity, 16, 78, 80, 87, 119
ontology, 27, 28, 29, 110
Oriental world, 7, 8, 42
Ouagadou-Bida, 112
Papaioannou, Kostas, xviii, 100
particularity, 6, 8, 19, 50, 51,
    63, 72, 75, 84, 88, 90, 110, 115,
    119
Pironet, Oliver
Plato, 69, 113
Polisario, xvi
power, 7, 9, 10, 13, 14, 15, 16, 19,
    20, 22, 25, 27, 33, 43, 46, 52,
    53, 56, 57, 59, 60, 61, 62, 72,
    80, 86, 87, 88, 91, 92, 94, 99,
    103, 107, 108, 110, 112, 116,
    123
praxis, 66, 67, 96, 111, 113
Présence Africaine, 27
primitive communism, 114, 116
proletariat, 56, 58, 61
Prometheus, 81, 83
private property, 9, 46, 55, 57, 57,
61, 110
publicity, 121, 122
Quillet, Pierre, xi
race, xviii, 13, 16, 22, 32, 38, 39,
    40, 42, 74, 100
rationality, xvii, 4, 34, 39, 47, 48,
    70
recognition, 13, 14, 47, 50, 52, 87,
    88, 93, 96
religion, xviii, 3, 13, 14, 16, 46, 57,
    58, 59, 60, 67, 81, 91, 100,
    101, 104
Ricardo, 97
Roman World, 9, 104
Rome, 7, 35, 49, 110
Rousseau, Jean-Jacques, 44, 45, 51,
100
Roux, Jean, 116
surculturalization, 123
Rwandan Genocide, xvi
Sahara, xvi, 34, 37, 38, 78, 118
Saharawi Republic, xvi
Sahlins, Marshall, 122
San Domingo Revolution, 98
Sarkozy, Nicolas, 32
savannah, 37, 66, 108

self-realization, 6, 31, 33
sensuality, 22, 23
Sépédokoté, Amadou, 112
Shields, Allan, 69
Sidibe, Modibo, 112
slavery, xv, 18, 19, 108, 109, 110,
    112, 114, 115, 116, 120
Smith, Adam, 96
social contract, 44, 45
SAP, 68, 69, 70
Solomon, Robert C., 54
Songhai, xv, 62
sorcery, 14
Soyinka, Wole, 69
Spanish Sahara, xvi
species-being, 80, 92
Sphinx, 42
spirit, ix, x, 1, 2, 3, 4, 5, 6, 7, 8, 9,
    10, 11, 13, 15, 16, 17, 18, 19, 20,
    21, 23, 24, 25, 26, 27, 28, 29, 31,
    32, 33, 34, 35, 39, 41, 42, 46, 51,
    52, 53, 57, 61, 65, 66, 68, 73, 79,
    80, 81, 82, 84, 96, 98, 103, 107,
    112, 120; Absolute, 4, 5, 6, 8, 11,
    21, 32, 34, 35, 51, 65
spirituality, 8, 10, 14
split, 1, 4, 8, 9, 10, 53, 59, 81, 82,
    84, 103, 105
Stace, Walter T., 98
state, the, xviii, 3, 4, 7, 8, 9, 10, 11,
    15, 16, 18, 19, 20, 23, 39, 43, 44,
    45, 46, 47, 48, 49, 50, 51, 53, 54,
    55, 56, 57, 58, 59, 60, 61, 62, 63,
    64, 65, 81, 82, 90, 96, 99, 100,
    101, 103, 109, 116, 117, 118
subjectivity, 10, 14, 20, 50, 51, 53,
    87
subsistence economy, 107
Sudan, 61, 115
Surrealism, 66
symbiosis, 66
Tavares, Pierre Franklin, ix, xii, 41,
    42, 98, 99
Tempels, Father Placide, 27, 28,
    29, 30
Terray, Immanuel, 120
Thompson, Robert, 68, 71
transcendence, 2, 4, 9, 47, 69, 92
Tuareg Rebellion, xvi

Touré, Samory, 108
Turnbull, Colin, xv, 115
unconsciousness, xi, 12, 20, 81
unity, 8, 13, 28, 29, 47, 48, 50, 51,
  53, 54, 58, 50, 66, 68, 7481, 82,
  84, 85, 87, 90, 113, 120, 121
universality, 5, 7, 8, 9, 11, 19, 20,
  40, 41, 49, 59, 72, 111
Victor, Gary, 99
violence, 9, 17, 19, 20, 23, 46, 66,
  96

vitale Force, 29, 66
Vogel, Susan, 68, 69
Wingo, Ajumé, 70
witchcraft, 13, 113
Wolof, 67
world history, xi, xviii, 3, 5, 8, 11,
  20, 36, 98, 101
Yartseva, Viktoria, 67
Yoruba, 68, 69, 71, 114, 115
Zaire, xvi, 29, 72

About the Author

Babacar Camara is associate professor of French and black world studies at Miami University, Ohio. He recently published *Marxist Theory, Black/African Specificities, and Racism.* His work has also been published in *Journal of Black Studies*, *CLR James Journal*, and *Research in Political Economy.* His research and teaching interests include Social, political, economic and historical analysis, modern African literature and cinema, cultural criticism, critical theory, French and Francophone literatures and cultures, African American and Caribbean Diaspora.

Dr. Camara received his baccalauréat in French and BA in English literature from the University Cheikh Anta Diop (Dakar, Senegal), his postgraduate degree in library, archive and information studies from the University College London (London, England), his MA degree in French and Ph.D. in comparative literature from the University of Rochester (NY).

CPSIA information can be obtained at www.ICGtesting.com
261080BV00002B/9/P

AM
891
.C36
2011